Hermetic America
Our Critical Heritage

Abraham Lincoln

Roger A. Weir

Shared Presence Foundation
Los Angeles, California
2020

Acknowledgments

The editors would like to express a deep gratitude to all those individuals who have committed their time to assist in editing and reviewing the text. Without your contributions we could not have fully realized this publication.

3rd ed.

Library of Congress Cataloging-in-Publication Data

A catalogue record for this book is available from the Library of Congress

ISBN: 978-1-7358769-2-4

Library of Congress Control Number: 2020925710

Foreword

These are a selection of lectures from a series entitled, *Hermetic America – Our Critical Heritage: James Fenimore Cooper, Abraham Lincoln, Henry Adams, and Mark Twain,* presented by Roger A. Weir in 1985. This series examines the creative persons who contributed to the development of America in the context of the vision of America as a land of free peoples.

The first Abraham Lincoln lecture – *Abraham Lincoln: The Wilderness Hero and His Spiritual Path to the White House* – is the fourth lecture in the series and was delivered on Thursday, April 25, 1985. The second Lincoln lecture – *Abraham Lincoln: The Civil War, Hermetic Unity, and the American Psyche Polarized* – is the fifth lecture in the series and was delivered on Thursday, May 2, 1985. The Shared Presence Foundation is excited that you are interested in these lectures.

info@sharedpresencefoundation.org

We are a not-for-profit organization dedicated to publishing works of historical, artistic, and scientific insight. Also we invite you to listen and read from thousands of lectures, transcripts, and more at:

https://sharedpresencefoundation.org

Table of Contents

Abraham Lincoln: The Wilderness Hero and His Spiritual Path to the White House

Presented Thursday, April 25, 1985

Abraham Lincoln: The Civil War, Hermetic Unity, and the American Psyche Polarized

Presented Thursday, May 2, 1985

❖ Our American Experience: A Matrix of Peoples – Lincoln's Focus and Melancholy – Lincoln's Greatness – The Election of 1860 – Lincoln Elected, Nation Formally Divided – Power Players Try to Control Lincoln – Lincoln's Intuition and the American Vision – Lincoln Offers to Pay the South to Free the Slaves – Caste Systems Preclude Understanding of Liberty – The Great Emancipator – Without Vision of Liberty, Man Seeks to Control – Opportunists in the Wings – The Civil War: Gruesome Modernity on Display – Lincoln and McClellan: A Troubled Relationship – America: An Experiment on the Verge of Extinction – Grant and Sherman Take the Mississippi Valley – Another Union Setback: Battle of Chancellorsville

❖ Lincoln's Great Speech: The Gettysburg Address – Lincoln's Practice of Government – Slides

List of Images, Illustrations, and Figures

Page numbers are indicated in brackets

List of Slides

Page numbers are indicated in brackets

Abraham Lincoln: The Wilderness Hero and His Spiritual Path to the White House

Presented by Roger Weir

Thursday, April 25, 1985

On Persons and Shapes of Meaning Over Generations

. . . I know that it's difficult to come in out of the wind and come into the realm of ideas, but at least there should be one place where we can come into the realm of ideas and not even ideas so much.

What we're attempting to do, patiently, week after week is to remind ourselves – because all of us know this – *remind ourselves that it is not the phenomenal world that we need to struggle to understand.*

We know the phenomenal world from running into it all the time, but we have all lived long enough and conscientiously enough to realize that *there are other shapes that exist also.*

And these are shapes of meaning, and they are not what we run into, but what we discover that we have been had by – too often.

And so, these shapes of meaning are what we are addressing ourselves to here on Thursday nights. And we have discovered over the last five years that we've been lecturing in this particular mode, and this is a mode, this is a style.

Rather than to speak upon a subject on a given evening, *we are attempting to extend out over a duration*, over a succession of dates, *a linking together of aspects of individuals* who were important and who continue to be important because those aspects of their lives link up with other aspects of their lives, and other aspects of others' lives.

Schooling us in the meantime – if we're patient about it, if we have continuity – schooling us to *a shape of meaning that seems to travel from generation to generation* and from person to person. It's remarkable that it should be so.

Individuals Can Understand Each Other

We are convinced in low moments of our lives that we're absolutely insular. How could anyone understand us and how can we understand anyone else? But the recurring awareness is that we do in fact, understand other people. And they do understand us and something passes from one to another and not only within a given generation, but a trans-temporality from generation to generation and sometimes leaping over generation so that the grandparent generations are close to us.

And **there are times when images of meaning and symbols of integration occur to us that have not made their appearance for sometimes hundreds of years** or in some cases, even several thousand years. These shapes of understanding, these meaningful configurations, have many names throughout history. We call some of the larger ones **archetypes** today, and we call some of the more continuous types reincarnation modes, or we call the amperage behind such a movement, such a dynamic, a karma, or perhaps an *élan vital*.[1] At any rate we recognize, in ourselves and together, that there are shapes of meaning that require of us a little bit of continuity and attentiveness just to discern and discover.

And we have on this particular Thursday night series this year, been addressing ourselves to **what is the shape of meaning of this country**.[2] Not in the sense of a political

---

[1] *Élan vital* is a term coined by French philosopher Henri Bergson (1859-1941) in his 1907 book *Creative Evolution*. In the English edition, *Élan vital* was translated as "vital impetus," but is typically understood to mean "vital force." It is a hypothetical explanation for evolution and development of organisms, which Bergson linked closely with consciousness – the intuitive perception of experience and the flow of inner time. (Wikipedia)

[2] The overarching title of the Thursday night series for 1985 was *Hermetic America* and comprises four sub-series of thirteen lectures.

doctrine and not in the sense of something that one would get from textbook summations in the bankrupt universities.

We are attempting to discern, *is there in fact an overriding shape of meaning to the largest context that we normally respond to in our everyday life*. And we are discovering now, we've gone far enough to realize that *there is in fact, a mysterious quality to the United States* and that this quality has not crept in unbeknownst to individuals, but has been *placed there conscientiously, time and again, patiently*.

We Can Refine Our Personal Qualities

We reviewed the life of *[Benjamin] Franklin* and we saw with what incredible arcane suavity *Franklin brought in the notion of the development of the person*, that a given human being has the capacity to grow, to educate oneself. And we need not stay in any condition that we find ourselves [in]. *We can in a word, better ourselves*, not in some sophomoric way, but in a very deep, profound way, transform ourselves. And that in this transformation, *we bring into the circulation of our personality, qualities that were not there before, and sometimes evoke qualities that were there, but were nascent, were not at all active*.

And we saw the development from Franklin through [Thomas] Jefferson, through [Henry David] Thoreau, through James Fenimore Cooper.[3]

And tonight, we come to Abraham Lincoln. And of Lincoln, perhaps the best statement that could have ever been made about him was made by one of his early biographers, Miss Ida Tarbell. She writes,

> Lincoln's greatness of mind, as well as the profundity of his understanding of the democratic scheme, come out finally in his attitude towards these efforts to hinder his policies. He of course had had political experience which made him expect the average man in the opposition to feel free to ridicule, thwart, and ruin his efforts. He was not their man. ***But I doubt if Lincoln could have realized how the silliness, obstinacy, selfishness, and vindictiveness which the party system arouses and justifies even in first-rate minds, would show themselves in men who were committed to him in the effort to save the Union.***[4]

---

[3] Roger delivered a series of thirteen lectures on Thursdays from January 3 – March 28, 1985 titled, *Hermetic America: Benjamin Franklin, Thomas Jefferson, Henry David Thoreau*. Within the *Hermetic America – Our Critical Heritage* lecture series, the current lecture was preceded by three lectures focused on James Fenimore Cooper.

[4] Ida M. Tarbell. *The Life of Abraham Lincoln*. Vol. 1. New York: Macmillan, 1924, p. xvii-xviii. Available online at the Internet Archive https://archive.org/details/lifeofabrahamlino1illtarb.

Spiritual Profundity Amid Participation in the Mundane

One of the outstanding qualities that Lincoln brings back into human history again, is the ability to grow in spiritual profundity while seeming to participate in what we call the external mundane world. Without taking himself out of the mundane world, Lincoln was able to offer an ever deepening pool of inner quietude, which was able to resonate increasingly and to bridge and amplify this spiritual resonance back out into the actual world, into those people who surrounded him, who ostensibly on the surface did not want to learn, did not want to be bridged to, did not want to change in the way that they found themselves changing.

An American Saint Francis of Assisi

But *Lincoln becomes an enigma in history*. In fact, if we could characterize him, in my estimation, *I think he's an American Saint Francis of Assisi*. And of course, 800 years in a different country would make a lot of changes. But he has the qualities that St. Francis had.

- The ability to make present before someone that mysterious certainty that there are purposes worth adhering to;
- That unity is a quality that belongs to the largest shape of meaning that human beings are capable of comprehending;
- And, that human efforts, social structures, societies, governments, communities, families must in some way,

echo or parallel this sense of unity in order to give themselves a sense of sureness and accuracy so that the good life is not only in terms of what one has, but in terms of the architectural orientation of what one is.

Synchronicity: Country Divides, Lincoln Arrives

And it is this capacity that *Lincoln manifests in this country in the moment in which it fell apart*, and the incredible accuracy with which Lincoln comes out of nowhere to the prominent center stage in the world at that time, is almost beyond what we would call normal circumstances. It's almost a synchronicity of epic proportions.

And we should remind ourselves here that the [American] Civil War [1861-1865] was not a small war. There were more deaths in the Civil War than there were in the Second World War for Americans. More than 500,000 Americans died in the Civil War.[5] There were more than 400,000 wounded as compared to about 400,000 killed in the Second World War and about 600,000 wounded.

---

[5] At the time of this lecture (1985) the death toll from the American Civil War was understood to be around 618,222 individuals. As a result of research from 2012, based on the analysis of census data, the estimate has been increased to be possibly over one million. Thus, the death toll from the Civil War is now generally expressed as a range: 618,222 – 1,000,000+. For some background information, see this New York Times article from 2012: https://nyti.ms/3mo6OwJ.

So, the *Civil War is the first great modern war. It is the first industrial based, technologically oriented war in human history. It is also the arcane result of the tremendous dynamic strength of the United States shifting from its initial unity to a polarity. And it is this movement towards a polarity that characterizes the American mind after the death of Jefferson to the election of Abraham Lincoln.*

From the mid 1820s until 1860, there was an increasing sense in the United States that everything could be changed; everything could be reformed; everything could be improved. And on the other side, everything could be a source of making money; everything could be developed; everything could be expanded. And so, the entire world was thrown open for grabs.

The United States Polarized by Power

It is in this time period, this 35 years from 1825 to 1860s, that the United States suffered an inflation, which if you would find in an individual, you would recognize as an illness not based on a neurotic, dis-recognition of themselves, but upon a psychotic perversion of themselves.

And the United States by 1860 had completely come apart in this polarity, that the sense of reality, the shapes of meaning had all constellated themselves on two sides of a central issue. And the issue was one of power – power for man. *The large manifestation of it was slavery, but the central issue should not be mistaken for it is of spiritual concern to identify that it was a question of power*, and it was this grabbing onto sources of increasing and almost unlimited, at least de-limited, power that polarized the United States from the 1820s until the Civil War. And of course, during the Civil War, it all came out.

We will find tonight, towards the end of the lecture, that *the trigger of the Civil War, of this polarity, was the admission of California to the Union in 1850. And that California finally broke open the delicate eggshell balance of power that had been set up.*

A Balance of Power is not Stable

And saying this, our ears perk up and our sense of history becomes attenuated because *the Civil War is the first time that we see visibly in modern history that <u>a balance of power does not work</u>*. And we today are told that in our lives, we must live in a balance of power. In fact, since most of us have been born and grown up, we have been told that the only way to live is in a balance of power.

American history in the 19th century shows that this is the most skittish of all worlds and leads to a perversion of all the shapes of meaning. So that instead of human right, it is human might that becomes the arbiter of structure and of achievement and of purpose. And we live in a world today that is being electrocuted by the sense of power.

Lincoln gives us an insight into how to deal with this. For he better than anyone in recent world history dealt with it accurately. And we will see this coming to the fore in his personality.

Lincoln's Early Life and a New Maternal Figure

Lincoln was born, as most of you realize, in Kentucky, South of Louisville.[6] And he was born in 1809. It seems that his father, Thomas, was a ne'er-do-well. From time to time he would own a few pieces of property and, from time to time, he would lose them.

Lincoln never felt very close to his father. He always felt a responsibility as a young man until he was 21 years of age to help out in the family, especially since *his mother had died when he was still fairly young, about nine*

---

[6] On Sinking Spring Farm near Hodgenville, LaRue County, Kentucky.

years old.[7] In fact, the second wife of Thomas Lincoln was a real angel for the two Lincoln children, Abraham and his sister, Sarah, who was about two years older than he.

Map of Lincoln's travels. Source: National Parks Service.

And when the stepmother came in a big wagon full of her furnishings and three children that she had had from a previous marriage – her first husband had died[8] – the first thing that young Abraham did was rest his head on her chest and she, taking his head in her hands, prayed for him. And

---

[7] Nancy Hanks Lincoln (1784-1818) was the mother of Abraham Lincoln, Sarah, and Thomas Jr. (died in 1812 shortly after birth). She died from milk sickness, also known as tremetol poisoning, which is a result of the ingestion of milk from an animal that has fed on the white snakeroot plant – which contains the toxin, tremetol.

[8] Sarah Bush Johnston Lincoln's first husband was a man named Daniel Johnston (1782–1816) and they had three kids together: John, Elizabeth, and Matilda.

The cabin where Abraham Lincoln was born near Hodgenville, LaRue County, Kentucky. Photographed after 1933 by Lester Jones. Source: Library of Congress.

Lincoln remembered this all the rest of his life – the saving grace of kindliness of love, the resolution that comes from the deepest companionship of all, the sympathy of the human heart. This impressed him enormously. And from that age on the cheerfulness of the stepmother tended to balance out the trauma of having lost his first mother.

Lincoln always carried with him a tone of melancholia, very deep, profound melancholia. There were times in his life when friends were almost afraid to talk to him, almost afraid to touch him, they would write that melancholy seemed to drip from him from time to time and he was almost unapproachable. And then there would be a slight change and Lincoln's satirical, playful personality would come into play and change, in the flash of a moment, the situation into one of frontier humor and delight.[9]

This quality of Lincoln's personality made him inscrutable to almost everyone at the time. Lincoln becomes in fact more and more mysterious as we trace his life and we will see some of the reasons for this.

Lincoln the 'Rail Splitter'

Lincoln grew tremendously, physically. He eventually would be six foot four, but would only weigh 180 pounds. So, he'd be tremendously stringy and wiry.

And from the time that he was about nine years old, he got very good at swinging an axe. The axe was the best tool of the

---

[9] For more details concerning Lincoln's melancholy, see *Lincoln's Melancholy: How Depression Challenged a President and Fueled His Greatness* (by Joshua Wolf Shenk, 2005).

Lincoln the Rail Splitter print by F. A. Schneider.
Source: Library of Congress.

American frontier. After the rifles were put down, it was the axe that was really the central tool and Lincoln's work with the axe was one of great artistry and stamina.

He is known in Lincoln Country as the rail splitter. And he really was that. He split enough rails and made enough fence to probably string several counties total. He got so good at this with his wiry form that he would often be left alone as a teenager to work out in the woods by himself. He could always be counted upon to bring his material home and to do his work. And while the young adolescent Lincoln was out in the forest, working with his axe, he would stop from time to time and just listen to the wind or just be with the forest.

The family had moved up into southern Indiana. They had gotten a little homestead there about sixteen miles up from the Ohio River in Spencer County. They had lived in a lean-to the first winter there and then Abe and several neighbors had built a small log cabin.

Lincoln's listening to the forest has a harmony to it that we'll find later on in American history. It's a little bit different from Thoreau. It's more like John Muir. For Lincoln, what came out of him was a feeling of untrammeled vastness. Not so much of the cosmos, but of life itself, of the potential of life. He could never go into a church service without feeling somehow cramped.

He never joined the church, although most of the family that he grew up with were members of various churches and various communities. But for Lincoln, there was a commitment – in this he is very close to Thoreau – there was a commitment to the ineffable and it was something that he did not dare tamper with. Even as a teenager, he realized that there was something real, alive, and loose in the world.

And from time to time, he would experience a whole series of setbacks and thinking it over in his frontier roughened way, he would realize that something was keeping him from doing certain acts. And again, he would realize that something was helping him to go in certain other directions. And Lincoln had an antenna out for this all of his life. And he always reserved within himself, the quality of wonderment. What could this be? Not so much who is this, but how does this come to touch me in this specific way again and again and again. And from time to time Lincoln would puzzle out daring little adventures for himself to see what would happen.

The Mississippi River Boat Adventure

For instance, when he was in his late teens – nineteen, twenty – it was decided that he and another friend would take this large river boat full of goods down the Ohio [River] to the Mississippi [River] and down the Mississippi, all the way to New Orleans. And of course, Lincoln being a very tough, mature youngster of about twenty years of age, it didn't seem too out of the way to trust this load to him.

And the reason he wanted to go was to see what was going to happen to himself. He wanted to see if you put me on these rivers and out there for three or four months, what's going to come out.

An etching showing flatboats on the Mississippi River at New Orleans. Source: "The Mississippi at New Orleans," an illustration by Alfred R. Waud, in William Cullen Bryant (editor), *Picturesque America*, vol. 1, New York: D. Appleton, 1872: p. 274.

Of course, there were some brigands who tried to take over the load from them. But Lincoln used all [six feet four inches of himself] to convince them that they'd be better off in the river than on his barge.

He was one of the best wrestlers around – let's face it. About the only time he was ever defeated was once during the Black Hawk Indian War.[10] Some champion wrestler from

---

[10] The Black Hawk War was a conflict between the United States and a group of Indian Nations, including bands of Sauks, Meskwakis, and Kickapoos led by the Sauk leader Black Hawk, that took place April 6 – August 27, 1832 in Illinois and Michigan Territory. In the Black Hawk

some other platoon beat him in two straight throws.[11] But that was about the only time that Lincoln ever lost a wrestling match.

Lincoln Witnesses the Evil of a Slave Auction

When he got down to New Orleans after having been on the rivers on the barge – sold the goods, sold the barge, made a handsome little profit for the owner of the barge and made good wages for himself – he stood there in New Orleans and the feelings came back to him and he realized that he was standing in front of a slave auction. And it was the first time that Lincoln had ever seen human beings sold. And he felt an eerie twinge of evil intent around the action. And Lincoln would tuck that into his personality and he would carry that with him, from thence forward.

War, Lincoln served as a volunteer in the Illinois Militia (as a Captain and a Private), April 21 – July 10, 1832.

[11] According to documented accounts, on April 22, 1832, in a wrestling match with Lorenzo Dow Thompson, Lincoln was thrown in two straight falls. The match was to settle whether Lincoln's company or Capt. William Moore's company would have the campground in Beardstown, Illinois. Notably, this was Lincoln's second day as a member of the militia ("April 22, 1832," *The Lincoln Log*, http://bit.ly/lincoln-wrestles).

"Slave Sale, Charleston, South Carolina," etching by Eyre Crowe.
Source: *The Illustrated London News* (Nov. 29, 1856): p. 555.

This riverboat or flatboat as you might call it, had been done for one of the richer men in the community, James Gentry.[12] And he was able to get back. They finally made their way back by horseback and on April 30th of 1827, Thomas Lincoln was able to finally finish paying for the 80 acres of the farm that he had set out to buy and no sooner had they gotten that paid off then they decided that they would move further North.

The movement in the Western, Midwestern part of America went from the South to the North. It wasn't a migration so much from East to West. That was true in Kentucky. And it was true in Pennsylvania. But, the movement in the American Midwest was from the South, North, so that there were Southern people constantly moving North. And about every five or six years, families would move another step further. And there would be families coming from the South, [replacing][13] them.

---

[12] "In 1828, he was hired by James Gentry, the richest man in the community, to accompany his son Allen to New Orleans in a flatboat loaded with produce. While there, Lincoln witnessed a slave auction on the docks. It was a sight that greatly disturbed him and the impression it made was a strong and lasting one" (Lincoln Boyhood National Memorial – NPS, "Abraham Lincoln's Boyhood in Indiana 1816 to 1830," https://www.nps.gov/articles/abraham-lincoln-boyhood-in-indiana-1816-to-1830.htm.

[13] Roger used the word 'displacing' but since the original families were moving of their own free will and were not pushed out the word 'replacing' seems to be a more accurate word choice.

Abe the Problem Solver

And by the time the Lincoln family moved to Illinois, they had moved to a community called New Salem. And Lincoln, sort of not knowing what to do with himself, decided to apprentice himself out to another flatboat that was going down the river – the Sangamon River runs into the Illinois [River] and the Illinois runs into the Mississippi [River] eventually.

And the man who watched him work saw Lincoln solve a very large problem. The flatboat had gotten caught about halfway over this dam and it couldn't go all the way over and they couldn't get it back. And so, Lincoln engineered getting some of the load taken on shore and the rest of the load put in the back of the boat so that the boat went out over the dam. Then he drilled holes in the bottom of the boat. And, a lot of the water that had gotten into it, leaked out and after plugging the holes, they moved the load to the front of the boat and it finally made it over the dam.[14]

---

[14] On a related note, in 1849 Lincoln invented a mechanism to be used for removing vessels from sandbars and shoals (Abraham Lincoln, "Manner of Buoying Vessels; or, Buoying Vessels Over Shoals" U.S. Patent #6469, https://patents.google.com/patent/US6469A ; Owen Edwards, "Abraham Lincoln Is the Only President Ever to Have a Patent," *Smithsonian Magazine* [October 2006], https://www.smithsonianmag.com/history/abraham-lincoln-only-presid ent-have-patent-131184751).

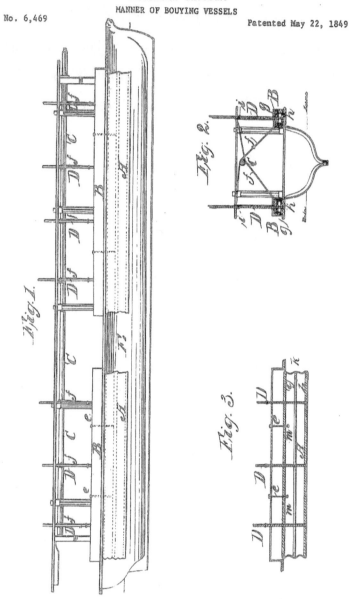

U.S. Patent #6469 – An illustration of the mechanism for which Lincoln was granted a patent. He is the only U.S. President to hold a patent.
Source: https://patents.google.com/patent/US6469A

And for this ingenuity, the man hired Lincoln to run a general store, and decided to open the general store there in New Salem. This is North of... it was North of Springfield.

New Salem disappeared in the late 1830s. There's a village there now, reconstructed of log cabins, which you could visit. And Lincoln's home is there, and a few other things.

Lincoln was immediately accepted into the town when he beat the town bully in a wrestling match. And in fact, all the other town bullies took a liking to Lincoln because not only was he tougher, but he knew more humorous stories. He'd been [to] places like New Orleans.

And so, Lincoln's humor began to come out and he began to compose poetry. I don't have very many samples here. Here's the kind of a little quatrain that Lincoln would write though:

> When first my father settled here
> T'was then the frontier line
> The panther scream filled night with fear
> And bears preyed on the swine

So, not very poetic, but it had a little bit of a character to it. Here's another little couplet from Lincoln's pen:

> Abraham Lincoln, his hand and pen
> He will be good but God knows when

He was just the most regular sort of lanky homely fellow. *He didn't drink and that was about the only thing that distinguished him from the rest of the rough frontier boys and young men*, but at everything else, he pretty well held his own.

The Long Nine and Illinois' 10th General Assembly

But as he was making his way, *Lincoln, for some reason, took out the papers and ran for an election for the state of Illinois and in the election, it was the first and only election that he ever lost on popular vote*. But the political bug bit him, and the next time an election opportunity came around two years later, he ran and he won.[15]

The capital of Illinois at this time was in Vandalia. It's a little tiny community today. And it was a very rough and rugged place. And Vandalia had probably about five or six thousand people at that time.

And the legislators were all very much like Lincoln himself – they were a rugged bunch. In fact, *Lincoln would begin to use his tremendous empathy with people*.

---

[15] Lincoln's first campaign for a position in the Illinois General Assembly was in 1832. In his second campaign, in 1834, he ran for the position of Illinois House of Representatives for Sangamon County (Wikipedia).

And the next election that came up, Lincoln managed to get a good many of his friends from Sangamon County elected along with him. In fact, all together there were nine [legislators][16] from that part of Illinois, and all of them were over six feet tall and they were called *The Long Nine* and they stuck together.[17] They probably all stood in a line and leaned about the same way against the door jams and spat about the same way. I don't think Lincoln spat.

But *The Long Nine* in a very casual way took over the Illinois state legislature. In fact, they took it over to the tune of wanting to move the state capital from Vandalia to Springfield because Springfield was the big up-and-coming town in their part of Illinois, north about 50 or 60 miles from Vandalia. And they realized that in trying to get this move to Springfield, they would have to have other people voting with them from other parts of the state. And the only way that you could get that done was the promise to do something for them.

---

[16] The Illinois General Assembly is the bicameral legislature composed of the state Senate and the state House of Representatives. Roger indicated 'Congressmen' but 'legislators' is more accurate since the nine members consisted of individuals from both sides of the state house.

[17] *The Long Nine* consisted of 7 state House members and 2 state Senators: John Dawson (House), Ninian W. Edwards (House), William Elkin (House), Job Fletcher (Senate), Archer Herndon (Senate), Abraham Lincoln (House), Andrew McCormick (House), Daniel Stone (House), and Robert Wilson (House).

So, Lincoln, who was the mastermind in this whole scheme, figured out that if we're going to try to get people from all over the state to vote to move [the state capital from Vandalia to Springfield] we're going to have to get a public works going for the whole state of Illinois.

Well, they made promise after promise and they designed to get roads and bridges and railroads. And when they got through it was going to cost the state of Illinois $10 million, which was a lot of money in the 1830s. But Lincoln proudly held up his trump card. He said, you know, the Erie Canal has paid for itself already and it cost much more than this.[18] And he said, I think Illinois will grow.

And of course, when they passed this appropriation bill newspapers all over Illinois claimed that property values had doubled overnight. And that this is going to be a boomtown. Every town was going to be a boomtown so that the whole state of Illinois started to look very attractive for investors.[19]

---

[18] The Erie Canal – which provides a waterway from the Hudson River to Lake Erie – was completed in eight years (1817–1825) at a cost of $7.143 million (Roger L. Ransom, "Canals and Development: A Discussion of the Issues," *The American Economic Review*, 54.3 [May 1964]: p. 375).
[19] The first bill passed by Illinois' 10th General Assembly was the *Internal Improvement Act* in 1837. It appropriated $10 million dollars in state funding for various improvements to the state's transportation networks. Months later a financial crisis struck the U.S. – known as the Panic of 1837 – which threw Illinois, and the nation, into an economic depression. Due to this unfortunate timing, Illinois took on major debt, amounting to $15 million. The state would ultimately take 45 years to pay it off (http://bit.ly/ill-10th-assembly-1837-act1).

And I think, you know, the rest of the story. Illinois bloomed like very few places did in the United States.

The first time that Lincoln went to Chicago in 1847, it had 16,000 people. It would be less than half a lifetime and Chicago would have a million people.[20]

And most of that design was due to the vision of Lincoln of seeing that the common frontiersman lacked only self-confidence. He saw it in himself that almost anything could be done.

Why, here it was! A man with less than three years of schooling. And he found himself the minority leader in the state legislature of Illinois at 25 years of age. Why, he was just filled with incredulity. Shucks, an American could do almost anything if you just give him an opportunity, that's all he needed. And he needed confidence.

And so, the development of the State of Illinois was the first visionary program of Lincoln. And they did get the capital moved. And in 1839 it opened its doors in Springfield. Springfield in those days was not anything to crow [about].

---

[20] In 1850 the city's population was approximately 30,000; by 1870 it was just under 300,000; then by 1890 the population grew to just under 1.1 million (National Academy of Sciences, *Growing Populations, Changing Landscapes: Studies from India, China, and the United States*, Washington, DC: The National Academies Press, 2001, p. 281 https://doi.org/10.17226/10144).

In fact, it was something to crow at.[21] Statements that we have from the time complain about the mud, there were no paved streets.

Remember, Springfield has good rich farmland which, when well-watered by the spring rains, which come every year, why it turns into mud if you don't plant something there. And I think the Springfield newspaper said, you know, we'd do better by planting rice since the streets are underwater most of the year. We could grow a nice crop here and sell it and make money. Except for the pigs, because the pigs were let loose and they roamed around the streets of Springfield grubbing up for things.

Lincoln one day was standing at the window and he muttered something as he saw this woman fall in the mud with her big plumed hat. And he said, "Rather like a duck. Feathers on top and down on the bottom." Springfield had 2,500 people at that time.

The Frontier Mode of Getting Agreement

But the wonderful quality of Lincoln was that he was able in his everyday homey way to plod through hour after hour, person after person, that it took to get a deal done. He knew

---

[21] Roger was making a distinction here, but he said 'crow at' in both sentences. The preceding sentence has been adjusted to end with 'crow about' in order to reflect the intended distinction.

how to lay back. He knew how to move forward. He knew how to hear what people really were after. He had an uncanny sense of what they were trying to say and what they would say, given half a chance and Lincoln found that he had an ability to create an opportunity for the other fellow to have his say exactly like he wanted.

And this was the secret of Lincoln's great charisma. You could always go and tell Lincoln exactly what you thought of him. You could criticize him. In fact, Lincoln took more criticism than almost any person I can think of, but he thrived on it because he was able finally to show, "well, now all of you are agreed in criticizing me. So, let's get together and work this thing out. And since I'm the butt of all these mis-affections, why don't we just plan to find some way to make this situation right so [you] don't have to complain about it."

He would work in that way. He had that kind of a quality. Rather than a leader, as someone who took charge, Lincoln evolved a frontier mode of getting other people to agree to work together so that they wouldn't have to put up with Lincoln anymore.

Lincoln's Romances

The romantic escapades in Lincoln's life are legendary because there are so few. Now it's said in all the early biographies and it's alluded to this day in legends in Illinois that the love of Lincoln's life was a young woman who died young, named Ann Rutledge, blue eyes and red hair, and kind of feisty and real pretty. But she had died at the age of 22 and that Abe was heartbroken ever after.

Mary Todd Lincoln, 1861. Photo by Mathew Brady.
Source: Library of Congress.

But investigation patiently into this has shown that Lincoln really didn't care too much about marriage. That is to say he was afraid of marriage and really didn't have to close an association with Ann Rutledge after all.

In fact, one of the closest associations he had was with a woman named Mary Owens. And he wrote her several letters from the legislature. And finally, when the deal fell through, as he told a friend of his, he felt pretty good about it since he said she really is too short for me and too plump for me and too loud.

And, you know, he married a woman just like that frankly. He married Mary Todd, and Mary Todd Lincoln was a little bitty woman. And she was feisty. She was the belle of the ball. She liked to – well now she had been to finishing school. She had grown up near Lexington, Kentucky. She was used to fine things – dances and clothes and more clothes and jewelry – things that cost a little bit. In fact, later on, it would become a *cause célèbre* in the White House when Lincoln would publish a disclaimer saying, I no longer am responsible for this woman's debts on clothes[22] . . . President.

He finally wrote her a letter just like he had written Mary Owens saying, I suppose that you won't have me. And I'm

---

[22] At the time of publication a reference for this statement was not found. For some details about Mary Todd Lincoln's shopping habits see: https://ehistory.osu.edu/articles/life-mary-todd-lincoln.

used to disappointment so you can tell me right now. And she said, well, the fact is I will have you, ornery as you are. And it sort of got through to Lincoln and he had what we would call a halfway nervous breakdown. He's going to have to go through with this thing. And on the 1st of January, 1843, Lincoln felt so sick that he couldn't go into the legislature battles.

He finally wrote Mary Todd and said, I just, I have to stand you up at the altar. I can't be there. And he said, I wanted to let you know, it was nothing personal against you. I just couldn't show up at the altar. Well, it took another eleven months before they finally did get married, but Lincoln never again had such an attack of melancholia as on the 1st of January, 1843.

In fact, Mary Todd Lincoln was very good for him. He did love her and [yet] he couldn't stand her constant yakking. And so, Lincoln began to figure out ways not to quite pay attention to what she was saying, but to pay attention enough so that if asked, he could say what she had said last. And so, Lincoln developed this fine tuned, split-ear – it's like a split-fingered fastball, you know, you can strike a lot of people out with it.

And Lincoln, like Benjamin Franklin before him, finally mastered the art of standing real still and calm while they lambast you. And after four or five hours, they'll get tired of this and they'll go on to other things and then you can go and do what you want. And he mastered that with Mary Todd.

This 2004 painting of Abraham Lincoln by Ned Bittenger is based on photos from 1847–1849 when he was a freshman member of the 30th Congress. Source: Collection of the U.S. House of Representatives.

Mr. Lincoln Goes to Washington

In fact, Lincoln, when he ran for Congress in 1846 and was elected, [he] was surprised.[23] And when he went to Washington [the] first time out, the first session of Congress was eighteen months after the election [which] set everything back for about a year.

We had quite a travail there and in December of 1847, when the Congress met, Lincoln right away discovered that he was a very good backroom dealer – that he could talk that talk, he could make the arrangements. And as a freshman Congressman, he was in great demand for going around and getting the boys together. And we call that today being a party whip.

Lincoln Speaks Out on Mexican War Inhumanities

But after two years in Washington, Lincoln felt somehow that he had had to stand up for the inhumanity of the United States against the Mexicans for having trumped up the war.[24] And he spoke out about it. And of course, all the veterans of the Mexican War in Illinois wrote letters to the [news]papers

---

[23] Lincoln ran as a Whig candidate.

[24] The Mexican-American War transpired between Mexico and the United States between 1846 and 1848. The war ended with the signing of the Treaty of Guadalupe Hidalgo which resulted in the United States taking over a portion of territory referred to as the Mexican Cession – which included California, Nevada, Utah, and parts of three other states, Wyoming, Colorado, and New Mexico.

and they decided they didn't want to support this kind of a fellow representing them in Congress and Lincoln didn't want to represent them.

And so, when the term was over, he went back to practice as a lawyer, went back to Springfield and he would spend five years, from 1849 to 1854, practicing his law and deepening his particular talent at listening, not so much to the forest now, but to the country, to the people in the country. He had tuned himself to the vast vision of the United States.

He'd been to Washington, he'd been to Boston, to New York, to New Orleans, and he had seen something and he didn't know quite what it was. And he was going to let that set in.

Well, let's take a break and let that set in for us, and then we'll come back for a little bit more...

Abe's Frontier Persona and the American Experiment

I'm having to skip over as usual, I outline about 40 or 50 things. And I realize that our time doesn't allow for that kind of detail. And it's a shame because Lincoln looks better in detail – the more detail, the better he looks.

He had a peculiar personality, as you must realize. One that was difficult to understand without the background that we've had so far. The openness of the American frontier was not an accident. It was not just a happenstance. It was planned for, it was made. It had been made conscientiously as early as the 1740s.

The personality of Benjamin Franklin was the first time that there's any kind of a mystical sense of the opening horizons. The wilderness before that had been seen as a problem, a source of terror. And from that moment on, there was an unrelenting desire in Franklin to kindle this sense of life into flame.

And it was Jefferson's genius to take that flame of the individuality of Franklin and amplify it, make it into a country. And it was the American character of the openness toward the world, toward possibility, toward what can happen that was in the air. And that individuals like Thoreau or Lincoln could tap into.

Someone like Thoreau never became conscious of that aspect. But we have seen that someone like James Fenimore Cooper became conscious of it when he went to Europe because he contacted there in long friendship, the Marquis de Lafayette[25] who said this age of revolution wasn't a

---

[25] Marquis de Lafayette (1757-1834), born Marie-Joseph Paul Yves Roch Gilbert du Motier and known as Gilbert du Motier in his home country of France (known in the United States simply as Marquis de Lafayette or even Lafayette) was a French aristocrat and military officer. Despite being a French subject, he fought against the British in the American Revolutionary War and also fought in the French Revolution.

revolution based so much on ideas, but upon vision and not on a vision of politics, but on a vision of man's nature, that Liberty in the form of Columbia[26] – the goddess of open spaces – was a new way to worship the divine.

Marquis De Lafayette, painting, 1822, by Ary Scheffer.
Source: National Portrait Gallery.

---

[26] Columbia, also known as Lady Liberty, is the female national personification of the United States.

Instead of huddling religion into closed spaces it was now going to be able to move dynamically in open spaces, going to become Homeric again, we're going to go for blue sky and sunshine, and this is going to be a new kind of a temple. And the temple will be the mobility of the people who are living lives in that reality.

'Columbia' as depicted in a cover illustration for the February 1928 issue of *The Elks Magazine* by Paul Stahr. Source: American Art Archives.

And so, the vision is to disclose that, and Cooper finally understood, began going back and reading his Jefferson, [and] was amazed at what was there. And then of course, when Cooper came back to the U.S. after seven years, he was astounded at how it was being maltreated. But the maltreatment of it is not all on the negative side.

Acceptance of Ideas by Way of Abuse, The American Way
Frank Lloyd Wright once, in a great sagacity, said *the American way is to finally accept ideas by way of abuse,* that when they kick it around long enough and it's still there, then they decide it must be pretty good. And they adopt it. And he says, *democracy will finally be accepted after all the abuses are heaped on it.* And it still survives. Then the mob will quiet down and get to work. And then we'll get something done.[27]

Lincoln had that kind of confidence in the largest sense, and in the particular sense. That is to say he was confident in the details and he was confident in the large vision. What he saw was that the problem was in the obstacles in the in-between scale of events, larger than the person and

---

[27] At the time of printing, the editor was unable to find a source for this statement attributed to Frank Lloyd Wright.

somewhat smaller than the universe. That it's that level, that's the obstacle.

And that from time to time, it seemed downright demonic that it would get in the way. And that man had to learn to either overcome this obstacle course, this obstacle level, through force or power, or realizing that trying to overcome it through force or power was just feeding energy into the obstacles. That the way to overcome it was to maneuver patiently in the detail, keeping the guiding star of the unity of the whole in vision. And that by this combination man could navigate himself free of the obstacles.

So that Lincoln trained himself increasingly in his life, not to pay attention to the problems, not to pay attention to the group levels where all the problems come up, but to look towards the individual, that human being and this human being, that they were the workable mobility in the world.

The American Individual is Free to Change

It was the individual person who was free to change, who was free finally to act. And that only by bringing individuals as themselves into play in a new way, could there be any kind of a collection called community, called a state, called a nation that could operate. He wouldn't have used the term, but he would have said, ***the problem is that the 'mass*** *mind' is against man and also against the universe*. It doesn't want either to win or to obtain; it doesn't want the individual, and it doesn't want the unity of all. It wants its own power plays, its own factions, which thrive on the fragmentation, which thrive on anesthetizing individuals so that they don't change their minds and so that they don't see the potential of the visionary unity of life.

Lincoln Sees the Ills of the Political Convention

And *the archetypal form that got in the way* in his time of the American individual and the American dream *was the political party system*. And it was not so much the political party system, but an invention, a form, a shape of meaning that came out of the political party system called the *political convention*. And Lincoln put his finger mentally on the political convention as the focus and the author of all of the travail that was coming to pass in his time that *the political convention took away the basis of grassroots democracy*.

Before then, and Lincoln had run for office before the conventions came in to stop it, anybody who wanted to could put himself up for an office. There might be thirteen to twenty-four to a hundred candidates for an office. Anybody who wanted to run would just post a notice and make some small payment for the forms. And they were in the race and whatever they could do, that was what they would do.

Individual Merit vs. Party Platform

But the political convention changed all that. It meant that there were going to be fewer candidates and they were not going to be candidates for themselves on their own merits, but they're going to be candidates for the party because now the party was going to back candidates, back them on the basis of a party platform.

And it was ***this party platform that filtered out the individual or toned the individual down or tuned the individual up to party expectations***. And it was ***the convention then that grabbed the jugular throat of the American dream***. And Lincoln was dead set against this, but he realized that this was the practical turn of events that in fact had happened.

And we're going to go into it a little bit more next week to see that when Lincoln helps found the Republican Party one of the things that will trouble him is the fact that it has to be done on a convention basis. And this will trouble Lincoln, to no end. It will be a problem that in his writings, he will say, "will have to be dealt with by the American people at some time in the future." That this is a real spiritual problem with the manifestation of Liberty, for individuals within a vision of unity. And that *political parties based on convention power are something that's going to stick in the craw of the American experience until it is gotten rid of.*

Human Bondage: A Chronic Spiritual Problem for Man

It's the same kind of problem that Franklin, toward the end of his life, and Jefferson at the beginning of his public career, both recognized in terms of slavery.

The writings of Franklin towards the end of his life in the early 1780s are filled again and again, with the observation that the problem of human bondage is a chronic spiritual problem for man and Jefferson will concur. And both of them will realize we can't do anything about it in our own time. That it simply is too deep, too broad in its ramifications to be tackled in our time, but that it will have to be dealt with at some future time.

And it's in Lincoln's time when that problem finally was dealt with. The problem that Lincoln saw for a future time [political party conventions] has not yet been dealt with.[28]

---

[28] Lincoln, as he expressed in a letter to John J. Hardin (U.S. Representative and militia general from Illinois) on January 19, 1846, was "satisfied with the old system" which, unlike the proposed convention system, did not afford any restriction on party candidacy (Lincoln to John J. Hardin, 19 January 1846, in Roy P. Basler (editor),

Although one individual will try, as we will see, and he will be politically crucified for it. And that man would be Woodrow Wilson.[29]

Vision Lost in the Jungle of Group Power Bargaining

So, Lincoln in his perception of spiritual form realized that it is in the area of bargaining or cooperating between people where all the trouble comes. And that in fact, when you add power to it, the ability to make decisions or to commandeer those grounds upon which decisions are made, power becomes, then, the negotiable reality for those forms, those middle forms. And *the individual doesn't have a chance in that jungle and the vision gets lost in that jungle*.

So, the problem increasingly for Lincoln was to find ways where he could operate as an individual himself within those forms. Still trying to maintain some basic contact with the reality of the vision of unity as a whole. And this is the poignant excellence of Lincoln as a human being that he

---

Collected Works of Abraham Lincoln, vol. 1, New Brunswick, NJ: Rutgers University Press: p. 356-357.

[29] In his first political campaign – for Governor of New Jersey – Wilson ran a campaign based on remaining independent from political party bosses – enforcers of party strictures – even though these bosses had been responsible for thrusting him forth as the party's candidate (August Heckscher, *Woodrow Wilson*, New York: Scribner, 1991: p. 214-215).

never gave up this quest and that he never ceased growing in capacity towards realizing that.

We can rarely profit from saying 'what ifs', but had Lincoln lived, the period after the Civil War would not have been as devastating as Reconstruction actually turned out to be. Lincoln was the only living person at that time who understood the intricacies of keeping the individual human being in touch with a universal vision.

There was no one who understood that – no one in the Office that is. We'll find that [Walt] Whitman understood this. And we'll find that [Herman] Melville understood this, but Lincoln was the only one who had any hope of realizing this.

Slavery becomes then one of these archetypal forms in between the individual and the vision that draws to itself increasingly like a whirlpool, all of the psychic energy, all of the economic concern.

Admission of California Triggers
Realization of Irreconcilability

And what had been a very delicate balance of power through the 1830s and the 1840s suddenly was triggered by the admission of California into the Union.[30] This was a

---

[30] California became the 31st state on September 9, 1850.

chronic problem at the time because it released the tender hold that both sides had upon seeing that they were still within the same ballpark, within the same country.

When California came in, it snapped the dream, ***it woke the polarized parties up to the fact that they were irreconcilable with each other and slavery as an issue***, not as an intellectual issue, but as a whole form of endeavor in between the individual and the universal had accrued to itself such massive power, mentally, psychically, economically, sociologically, that the South was convinced that it could not survive without it. And the North became convinced that it could not survive with it. These were the constellated precipitated polarities that came up.

It was understood at the time that this was going to happen. And so, everything that could be done in the United States Congress at the time was mooted together. There was a famous Proviso from David Wilmot of Pennsylvania in 1846 in the autumn before everything became apparent. Texas had come into the Union and it became apparent that one more large state like this and the whole balance was going to go haywire. And so the *Wilmot Proviso* had introduced a resolution, and this is a quotation from the resolution,

That as an express and fundamental condition to the acquisition of any territory from the Republic of Mexico by the United States, by virtue of any treaty which may be negotiated between them . . . neither Slavery nor involuntary servitude shall ever exist in any part of said Territory.[31]

Now, of course, the resolution was never passed.

The Fugitive Slave Law of 1850

When California came into the Union, there was a need to make some kind of a compromise and the Compromise of 1850 balanced all of the demands and needs for the polarized sides.[32] But the one quality that was left wild was called the Fugitive Slave Law.[33] And that was that slaves fleeing, trying to get free – and remember, now, this would not be fleeing

---

[31] The so-called *Wilmot Proviso* was an amendment to a congressional bill proposed by President James Polk to pay for land from Mexico as a result of the Mexican-American War. There were two versions of the Proviso. The excerpt referenced here is from the 1846 version. Notably, the text of the *Wilmot Proviso* was directly influenced by Thomas Jefferson's text for the *Northwest Ordinance* (1784).

[32] The Compromise of 1850 was a package of five separate bills passed by the United States Congress in September 1850 that defused a political confrontation between slave and free states on the status of territories acquired in the Mexican–American War. It also set Texas's western and northern borders and included provisions addressing fugitive slaves and the slave trade (https://en.wikipedia.org/wiki/Compromise_of_1850).

[33] The Fugitive Slave Law, also known as the Fugitive Slave Act, was passed by the U.S. Congress in 1850 as part of the Compromise of 1850. The Law resulted in the assessment of fines and jail terms for any individual aiding or abetting a runaway slave, and also implemented rules that punished federal marshals for inaction when dealing with any person potentially considered a runaway slave (https://spartacus-educational.com/USASfugitive.htm).

out in the open, there were 'underground paths', just like there are leading from tyrannies to free nations now – there are ways to get out and these paths are the various families.

Thoreau's family was one of these families. It had little links and underground stations all through the North helping Blacks to get up to Canada or helping them get new identities and get settled out in the countryside.[34] The Fugitive Slave Law said, if you help a slave you are guilty of a crime that is punishable. You will be thrown into prison; you will be fined. And if you continue in this, you will be executed.

The Fugitive Slave Law struck down at the whole basis of the humanity of helping slaves to gain their freedom. And it was the Fugitive Slave Law that came into effect in 1850, that made it impossible for anyone ever again, to believe that there could be a reconciliation.

Every time an incident came up, the families that would be caught – I think we've seen the same thing in this country with the Salvadorians and with the people from Guatemala – that if you help them now you're committing a crime, you're culpable for this. Well all this was within the United States itself, and it completely shattered the vision of the Union.

---

[34] These 'underground stations' are commonly known as the "Underground Railroad."

'Them and Us' Attitude Shatters Unity

There was no longer any such thing. There was increasingly a 'them and us' attitude on both sides and because of the rise of economic power [in the North]. Remember now the United States was industrializing at a tremendous pace. Look at the growth of Illinois itself. In the beginning of the 1830s, it was wilderness. By the 1860s, 30 years later, it was one of the most populous States and it was already an industrial power. By the 1880s, Chicago would become one of the industrial centers of the world, all within a period of a very short human life.

This rising industrial might flowed into this polarity and it just energized and exacerbated the situation. And so that every year during the 1850s was more and more of this electrocuting tension in the American psyche, and the Civil War is this nightmarish waking up to the intolerable conditions that had come to bear upon the mind of the time.

Lincoln was the only individual in a position to do something about this in terms of the massive unity of it all. There were individuals who could do something for themselves.

Whitman's Finding of Individual Compassion

[Walt] Whitman during the Civil War became an attendant in hospitals, nursing the sick and wounded. And we'll see when we get to Whitman, in *Drum-Taps*,[35] the incredible compassion that he finds, not from looking at the situation as a whole, but in tending, person after person after person, hundreds of people after hundreds of people, all on an individual basis, until it added up brick by brick to a structure of compassion that he could no longer deny was a necessary part of the universal self, that compassion is as real as anything could possibly be, but it was on the individual basis.

The only other individual at the time – and we'll see this – who tried to grasp the universal overall vision of it was Herman Melville. And what he came up with is that man is increasingly confronted with the possibility that at his core is evil. And progressively with *Moby-Dick*, with *Pierre; or, The Ambiguities*, with *The Confidence-Man*,[36] Melville will become closer and closer to the contention that Job had, only in a negative way. That God must be called to account to

---

[35] *Drum-Taps* (1865), is a collection of poetry written by American poet Walt Whitman during the American Civil War (Wikipedia).
[36] *Moby-Dick; or, The Whale* is an 1851 novel by Melville. *Pierre; or, The Ambiguities* is the seventh book by Melville, first published in 1852. *The Confidence-Man: His Masquerade*, first published in 1857, is the ninth book and final novel by Melville.

have allowed a universe like this to have come into being. And Melville himself will be driven finally, in the 1870s to go on a personal pilgrimage to Jerusalem, to try and resolve for himself, this situation.

Lincoln was the only individual who had a vision of the whole and knew how to get there personally, individually. And so, it is one of the most miraculous synchronicities in history that Lincoln decides to go back into politics in 1854 – decides that he will go back into national politics and will take with him this sense of profundity that he found that he was able to work with. And Lincoln arriving in Washington in 1854 will be one of the most miraculous situations of all.

The second time that Lincoln ran for office as a youngster, one of his opponents was Steven Douglas.[37] And it'll be interesting to see that over a period of some twenty-some years, that when it would come down to the presidential election, Douglas would again be one of his opponents.

It's one of those earmarks that hermetic questers get used to seeing again and again: that there are telltale signs of some universal flower unfolding because all the petals have this particular shape, this particular tone and color, and there they are again. And it's an indication that this situation

---

[37] In 1858, Lincoln and Douglas faced off for the same U.S. Senate position; Lincoln ultimately lost the race to Douglas.

is part of a whole blossoming. And Lincoln will be attentive to that.

Douglas incidentally was little, he was about five feet, but he had huge shoulders that could hardly get through a door and a mane of hair and he loved to argue and thrash his hair around. And one time Lincoln's first law partner, a man named Stuart,[38] got tired of Douglas ranting and raving, and grabbed him by the nape of this bull neck, and started carrying him off from the speaker's platform and Douglas bit the man's finger and he carried teeth marks for the rest of his life. And Lincoln, of course, just observing all this, made up some comments about Douglas' reckless mouth.

We'll see some more of Lincoln next week.[39]

---

[38] John T. Stuart (1807–1885) first met Lincoln during the Black Hawk Indian War (they served in the same battalion). Stuart was also from Kentucky and was a trained lawyer who also served as a U.S. Representative for Illinois. Lincoln and Stuart were law partners between 1837 and 1841 (Wikipedia and *Biographical Directory of the U.S. Congress, 1774–Present*).

[39] The second lecture on Lincoln was delivered on May 2, 1985. The text of this lecture is included on the following pages.

Abraham Lincoln: The Civil War, Hermetic Unity, and the American Psyche Polarized

Presented by Roger Weir

Thursday, May 2, 1985

Our American Experience: A Matrix of Peoples

We come back to Lincoln tonight. And we come back to the elusive fulcrum of the American experience. And sometimes it's better to call it the American experience rather than American history.

Other peoples have a history, we do not. The French people are French. They have a French history. The Italians are the Italian race. They have an Italian history.

But the United States is a collection and a matrix of all nations. And it has an experience and not a history. And this makes it very elusive. It means that the least interesting subject in the world is American history, because if you look at it in terms of a static, linear development it doesn't add up.

And the corollary to that is that every generation tends to dismiss the previous generations. They're not forefathers so much as old fashioned. And this is our problem.

The American mind renews itself every nineteen years. Just like [Thomas] Jefferson hoped it would. And every new generation figures the other ones have done all right for their time, but it's time for them to move over. That's the basic standpoint.

You never find that, you never find a Frenchman saying, we're just not going to do things the way that they've been done before. They are proud of Charlemagne. They are proud of Napoleon. They are proud of Le Grande Charles.[40] And they're French. And the next generation is going to learn to be French. This is true in any country. It is not true in this country.

So, we have a very peculiar situation. And the only way in which to get a grip upon the American experience is to go to the individuals – the people. The only reality in the American experience is the people. And this is esoteric. This is as esoteric as you can get, because it means that the only focus for reality is in the people. And that if you slide your emphasis to something indirect, like a doctrine or a philosophy, you miss the American experience. You come out with 'what ifs', or what could be.

And thus, there is no religious, no political, no philosophic unity that can be grasped and held up and be said to be the substrata for American thought.

---

[40] Charles De Gaulle (1890-1970), also known by the nickname 'Le Grande Charles', was a French army officer, statesman, and ultimately the President of France from 1959-1969.

This in the past, in the recent past, proved to be a bugbear because individuals were still attempting to write histories of American thought, histories of American philosophy. And have you ever read any of them yourselves? No one has.

When we get to someone like John Dewey who will investigate and try to find out what is the history of American thought, he will set it aside. He'll say the only focus is the moving present. And that a logic for this kind of mind is not a category of arrangement on the basis of an existing order, but a sheer probing in a process of inquiry to find out what is possible. And he'll call it pragmatism. And he'll say, this is what we have.

And so, the American experience focuses itself in individuals. Whatever American history might be, it only occurs, its only focus in reality is in people – individual human beings.

And this was done on purpose. This was made by design. It was tailored as we have seen by [Benjamin] Franklin and Jefferson, largely, and brought into being so effectively that it worked even sight unseen. Even an individual like Henry David Thoreau we found, who had absolutely no contact with Franklin and Jefferson, lived purely in the American experience. He was an atemporal sage. And his responsiveness was to what we would call 'nature as such'.

And he would say the history that I'm interested in is the life cycle of this pine tree, or of this squirrel, or of this river.

He was a naturalist and you have to put that word in neon lights. He was a naturalist like the old Daoists were naturalists. He was a human being like the old Upanishadic gurus were human beings. They were of cosmic nature. And they had no attentiveness whatsoever to the cloud-like phantom doctrines that the mind engenders to cover itself and give itself stability. That *the American experience finds its stability in a dynamic appreciation of the present.* And finds its character in the multidimensionality of the possibilities of that present.

The most popular ad for the most popular American product says, "Coke is It." They don't tell you the recipe; they don't tell you anything. Even though they've changed the recipe. It's IT. This is IT. IT is real. And that's all you need to know. Buy IT.

In a sense, *Americans only buy reality.* The problem is, *from time to time not having a doctrine to refer to, not having any categorical litmus test of certainty, they choose all kinds of strange realities.*

It devolved upon Lincoln in his time to find the real thread, the real continuity, and to hold onto it Job-like. Almost like the military request in the Second World War to those who held the Remagen bridge[41] – hold until relieved. When that will be, we're not sure. But however long it is, you have to stay there. Lincoln's presidency was like that.

Lincoln's Focus and Melancholy

And we discovered last week – a peculiar characteristic of Lincoln – that *he could hold in simultaneous focus the individual and the cosmic at the same time.* The overall vision, the master vision, and it had direct access down to the individual. And he had trained himself, largely unconsciously at first, but increasingly conscious about the depth and profundity. He had trained himself to ignore the middle ground.

This is why Lincoln's humor is always earthy. It's always peculiarly frontier-style humor. And why the humor comes spontaneously out of an overwhelming melancholy. That *the general tone of Lincoln's personality was described by contemporaries as being unbearably melancholy*. Dripping with this melancholy. This melancholia is not depression. It has nothing to do with depression.

---

[41]   This is a reference to the Ludendorff Bridge (in German, Ludendorff-Brücke) – a railway bridge spanning the Rhine River located near Remagen, Rhineland-Palatinate, Germany.

Melencolia I, 1514, engraving by Albrecht Dürer.
Source: Wikimedia Commons.

Albrecht Dürer in the High Renaissance did the most esoteric of all prints called *Melencolia I*. Where it showed the Angel of Deliverance sitting with his chin on his fist and surrounded by all the new instruments of man's confidence that he could understand the world and himself. It is this kind of esoteric melancholia that Lincoln had.

And it has an underside, which comes out poignantly in the individual who is free. So that liberty occurs in an individual and in the whole, but rarely occurs in between. And so, the problem is, how to manifest, how to bring liberty out of an individual, amplify it to others, or how to bring liberty out of the universe, brought into others.

The cosmos and the individual get along very easily. It's not always, in fact, it's quite rare that it happens. But when it does happen, the mystic and the cosmos hum together in silence very, very easily. But occasionally there needs to be someone for whom the capacity is there to transmit this from below and from above simultaneously in order to make a linkup happen that is in jeopardy. And Lincoln was that individual. But he occurs within this mysterious matrix – the American experience. And so, he is the most elusive of all figures in history.

Lincoln's Greatness

It is very difficult to see and understand why **Lincoln is great.** And he is great like Augustus Caesar was great. He is great like Scipio Africanus is great. He is one of the great figures of world history. Because he occupies that most incredible of all barbells. ***He holds the integrity of the individual and the integrity of a universal vision of liberty, simultaneously, in a time where both were being torn apart and discarded because the fantastic shapes in the middle were trying to usurp the focus.*** Trying to become the essential nature.

Campaign advertisement for Abraham Lincoln and Hannibal Hamlin, the Republican ticket for the presidency in 1860. Lithograph by William H. Rease. Source: Library of Congress.

The Election of 1860

Lincoln reemerged on the national scene in the most peculiar circumstances. If you recall, he had been to Congress and then had come back to Illinois. Back to Springfield. Set up a law practice. And then stayed there in Illinois.

As the election of 1860 was coming to the fore, the polarity pressures in the United States had reached a breaking point and it actually pulled apart. And so, ***the election of 1860 was a case in point for all the various factions that had been already separated.***

The South psychologically had already separated itself. But the South had separated itself in terms of the individual states. You know they did not all secede at the same time. The first was South Carolina. At which somebody quipped "it's too small to be a Republic and too large to be an insane asylum."[42] And then the other states dribbled after it in order. And it took some while, many months for this to happen.[43]

---

[42] James L. Petigru (1789-1863; lawyer, politician, and jurist) from Charleston, South Carolina made this statement after South Carolina seceded from the Union in 1860.

[43] The Confederate States seceded from the Union, over a six month period, in the following order: South Carolina (Dec. 20, 1860), Mississippi (Jan. 9, 1861), Florida (Jan. 10, 1861), Alabama (Jan. 11, 1861), Georgia (Jan. 19, 1861), Louisiana (Jan. 26, 1861), Texas (Feb. 23, 1861), Arizona Territory (Mar. 16, 1861), Arkansas (May 6, 1861), Virginia

But before the election of 1860, the South had decided that their candidate was going to be a man named [John C.] Breckenridge.[44] And on the other side, Stephen Douglas,[45] who was a tremendous orator, but who of course ran up against the laconic universal wit of Abraham Lincoln in a series of debates. But there was Douglas and there was Breckenridge and there was Lincoln. And there [were] a few others in the hopper, but they really didn't count.

Lincoln Elected, Nation Formally Divided

When the election was over, Lincoln did not win in terms of popular vote. But because of the arrangement of the Electoral College, Lincoln won by a great margin. For instance, he had 173 electoral votes to Stephen Douglas' 12.[46] And Douglas outpolled him in the popular vote.[47] This was

---

(May 23, 1861), North Carolina (May 20, 1861), and Tennessee (Jun. 8, 1861).

[44] John C. Breckenridge (1821-1875) was a politician from Kentucky who served in both houses of Congress, was the 14th Vice President in the James Buchanan administration (1857-1861), and then also was the Secretary of War for the Confederate States.

[45] Stephen A. Douglas (1813-1861) was a politician and lawyer from Illinois who, among other things, served as a Senator and Representative in the U.S. Congress.

[46] Lincoln and his running mate Hannibal Hamlin actually won 180 electoral votes. Breckenridge and his running mate Joseph Lane captured 72 electoral votes. John Bell and his running mate Edward Everett secured 39 electoral votes. Douglas and his running mate Herschel V. Johnson won 12 electoral votes.

[47] Lincoln actually achieved a plurality of the popular vote by capturing 39.8% of the votes. Douglas captured 29.5%, Breckinridge got 18.1%, and

proof positive to the states in the South that the Union was no damn good. These politicians have a hold upon the situation. Why should we even mess with it? [These are] the kinds of thoughts that were happening in the South. And if you read in the writings of Jefferson Davis[48] – which a good friend of mine made available to the Whirling Rainbow library[49] – he's an extraordinarily intelligent man. Very capable of thinking through something. And if you thought in any terms less than the unity of the nation as an esoteric commitment to reality, Jefferson Davis was right. All the arguments of the South were correct. They were poignant assessments of what had gone wrong with the governmental structure.

It was increasingly dominated by greedy cliques of Northern industrialists. The only difficulty was that the South complained not on the basis of there being greedy cliques of Northern industrialists so much as the fact that they were Northerners.

Bell got 12.6%. Lincoln achieved this while not even being on the ballot in 10 Southern States (Wikipedia).

[48] Jefferson F. Davis (1808-1889) was most famous for being the one and only President of the Confederate States from 1862-1865.

[49] Whirling Rainbow was located at 2029 Hyperion Ave, Los Angeles, California and served as Roger Weir's residence and presentation venue for a number of years during the 1980s and early 1990s. The library, comprising more than 30,000 volumes in 1985, served as a resource to support Weir's work and complement his presentations.

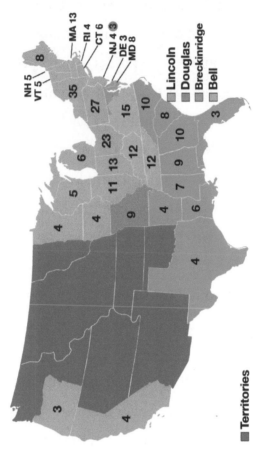

A map showing the Electoral College results of the 1860 Presidential election. Source: Wikimedia Commons.

We [the South] have our own greedy cliques and they would like to have their share of the pie, which they're not getting. Therefore, we're going to split on this basis. And the reaction to that in the North was that, we are controlling the situation and you will darn well behave. And in this polarity, which was the perfect split, the perfect egotistical split, there was almost no one who saw the truth of the matter. Who saw the thread of continuity, the reality of the experience.

Power Players Try to Control Lincoln

And Lincoln did and this is why he is one of the world's greatest figures. Because *he was able in a time of an absolute junkyard of fragmentation to accurately conceive the truth, to accurately present himself as a forward, honest individual in contact with this vision of liberty and to maintain that, individually, single-handed, against all comers*. Because as soon as Lincoln was elected, everybody tried to control him.

One of the individuals who thought he was going to be elected was William Seward. I think he was governor of New York.[50] Very powerful man at this time. And he became Lincoln's Secretary of State because he had a lot of clout and you had to put individuals like this into office. And Seward thought, this country-bumpkin lawyer, I'm going to tuck him in my back pocket. Now, let's see what I want to do with this country. So, *Lincoln was surrounded – <u>he was an island in an ocean of greed</u> – and he had no one to turn to*. And you can't call Mary Todd Lincoln someone to

---

[50] William H. Seward (1801–1872), of New York, was the 12th Governor of New York (1839–1842), U.S. Senator from New York (1849-1861), and then U.S. Secretary of State (1861-1869).

turn to. I mean, if she was out for a shopping spree, you could turn to her.

Lincoln's Intuition and the American Vision

But in these tremendous pressures Lincoln was able to pivot and hold himself accurately in his cognizance and never lose track of where he was. This is a very esoteric thing. This takes Hermetic navigation, because you don't have any coordinates that you can trust except your own, what we would call intuition. And your intuition has to be responsive to something.

And for Lincoln, his navigation was responsive to the guiding star of the overall conception that *this nation was not a nation-state, but was a vision of the prototype of the unity of humanity.* That the universal self of mankind as a whole was projecting and manifesting itself here. And that this was the cradle for mankind's salvation. Not as a new Jerusalem in the old sense. But in Whitman's words, coming out of the cradle and gently rocking and needing to have a little bit longer incubation. That what was wrong was that we had not solved some of the basic problems.

And Lincoln with unerring accuracy decided that the asymmetrical polarity generated itself out of a primordial inequality called slavery. That, that was the true reason, the true focus of why the American experiment had gone wrong. Why there wasn't unity and why there was polarity. Why there was all this tension.

Now there had been abolitionists for decades. You remember when we talked about [Henry David] Thoreau? That Thoreau's aunts and mother and all were part of a whole sequence of individuals who spoke out against slavery. Who put an underground railroad in for slaves to make their way from house to house and get up free to Canada and all of this. But there was no one who had seen that it was an essential point. That it was a focus of reality that, in fact, fractionated the unity.

And Lincoln put it succinctly that this country is founded upon the premise that all men are created equal. And that that is not a political platitude but is a religious insight that cannot be abrogated. And that the abrogation of it in any single way, abrogates the unity of the whole. And that this was not being understood.

[No. 26.] Joint Resolution declaring that the United States ought to coöperate with, affording pecuniary Aid to any State which may adopt the gradual Abolishment of Slavery. April 10, 1862.

Be it resolved by the Senate and House of Representatives of the United States of America in Congress assembled, That the United States ought to coöperate with any State which may adopt gradual abolishment of slavery, giving to such State pecuniary aid, to be used by such State in its discretion, to compensate for the inconveniences, public and private, produced by such change of system.

APPROVED, April 10, 1862.

The United States should aid any State in the gradual abolition of slavery.

Congressional Joint Resolution for national compensated emancipation. *United States Statutes at Large*, vol. 12 (1859-1863): p. 617. Source: HathiTrust Digital Library.

Lincoln Offers to Pay the South to Free the Slaves

And so, Lincoln conceived of a tremendous plan, in his mind, of a way in which he could undo this thirty-year span of travail. And the handle on it was freedom for the slaves. And his overall strategy was something like this:

The slaves are owned by individuals and the individuals control these states. And so, these states have become essentially the middle ground projection of the unity of all these slave holding peoples. So that the structure of any of the Southern States, the sovereign independent State of Alabama, the sovereign independent State of South Carolina, had its sovereignty and had its independence really on a group projection of its ability to own slaves and run this slave-based economy.

And so, *Lincoln conceived of a plan whereby the federal government, the United States as a whole, would acquire those slaves from the individuals by way of the states.*[51] *And then the federal*

---

[51] In a letter to Congress, Lincoln recommended the adoption of a "Joint Resolution" which "Resolved that the United States ought to cooperate with any state which may adopt gradual abolishment of slavery, giving to such state *pecuniary aid*, to be used by such state in its discretion, to *compensate* for the inconveniences public and private, produced by such change of system" (Abraham Lincoln, "Message to Congress; March 6, 1862" in Roy P. Basler (editor), *Collected Works of Abraham Lincoln*, vol. 5, New Brunswick, NJ: Rutgers University Press, 1953: p. 144-147). This Joint Resolution was based on a bill that Lincoln had drafted for compensated emancipation in Delaware in 1861 (Abraham Lincoln,

*government, owning all the slaves, would then
choose not to re-sell them to anyone and thus bring
to a close this sore spot, this open flaw.*

This was seen intuitively by the South as a danger to them,
worse than any kind of military or industrial takeover
because it pulled the tooth. There was no longer going to be
any possibility. The South could not run its economy without
slaves. The Southern mind could not hold the stability, which
it had engendered for itself – sociologically, psychologically,
as well as [economically]. The Southern mind had become
habituated to this layering. And this is an endless
habituation.

Caste Systems Preclude Understanding of Liberty

Look at how many gurus India has had and the caste
system is still there. I mean, the untouchables in 1965 had to
all convert to Buddhism *en masse* because there was no
chance ever to get rid of the untouchability. **This caste
system, in fact, becomes an indelible stain upon the
psychological structure of the individual.** And that's
what's wrong with it. It's not just the sociological and
economic injustice, which is external; it's the fact that it

"Drafts of a Bill for Compensated Emancipation in Delaware" in Roy P.
Basler (editor), *Collected Works of Abraham Lincoln*, vol. 5, New
Brunswick, NJ: Rutgers University Press, 1953: p. 29-31).

stains the personal structure of reality, skews it so that they cannot understand liberty. They cannot understand the integrity of an individual. **They cannot understand the vision of a unity of the people.**

One could say to them **that we are strong because we are a people together.** And **they would interpret that as a political statement.**[52] And then say, well, we don't agree with you. This group over here, we think this way, you think the other way. They cannot understand liberty and unity. They cannot understand equality. Because this is a psychological skew that is within the person and manifests itself in the society because it comes out of those individuals.

Without Vision of Liberty, Man Seeks to Control

Now, if they can't understand the unity of the country, they place the unity of their state, which they control, which is just another projection of themselves. And they say on this basis, we can continue to live and operate. And this was the essential falsity that Lincoln was able to see through with almost no one to corroborate his insight.

---

[52] In this context, "they" refers to someone with a skewed psychological perspective as a result of being a slave owner or caste member, from which they cannot understand the vision of liberty and unity as something beyond a political statement.

He offered the South en masse many times and its administration the chance to have the federal government buy at the going price all of the slaves there were. How many do you have? How much do you want for them? We will pay you for them.[53]

So, it was not a question of Lincoln not trying; it was not a question of Lincoln not being able to come up with a workable plan. It was the fact that he was standing alone and there was almost no way to amplify his effectiveness as an individual to large groups.

And it took almost the whole course of the Civil War for him to find a way to reach the American people. And the genius of Lincoln was that he was able to find a way to do that. He not only held himself in that spiritual position, unstinting for all those years. And not only conceived and saw the vision of the unity as a whole, but he brought the American people back to where they could get in touch with that again, by the millions.

---

[53] One such time resulted in a Congressional "Joint Resolution" which was passed by Congress on April 10, 1862. The text of this Resolution has been included in this booklet and is also available here: https://babel.hathitrust.org/cgi/pt?id=mdp.35112200623611&seq=655.

The Great Emancipator

He is the 'Great Emancipator' not just of emancipating slaves, but of emancipating the American people from a skewed polarity of vision that made it impossible for them to continue the experiment. There wasn't going to be any more experiment if he did not succeed.

And Lincoln's greatness also lies in the fact that he was able to do this Herculean task in a time when the country was simply decimated by the Civil War.

We mentioned last week that over a half million Americans were killed in the Civil War in a 4-year period.[54] Another 300,000 wounded. And you have to understand that wounded doesn't mean Band-Aids. In the Civil War days they amputated all the time, so that probably two-thirds of the wounded were amputees. And these figures don't take in the civilian debt. They don't take in the civilians displaced. The population of the U.S. was only eighteen million.[55]

---

[54] At the time of this lecture (1985) the death toll from the American Civil War was understood to be around 618,222 individuals. As a result of research done in 2012, based on the analysis of census data, the estimate has since been increased to be possibly over one million. The death toll from the Civil War is now expressed as a range: 618,222 – 1,000,000+. For some background information see: https://nyti.ms/3mo6OwJ.

[55] The population of the United States of America in 1860, based on the Census of 1860, was approximately 31 million people. After the secession of the Confederate States, the population of the Union States totalled

Can you imagine? Can you imagine thirty or forty million people today being killed or maimed in a four-year period? And this was at a time when the United States was very precarious.

Opportunists in the Wings

It was during the Civil War that the French sent Archduke Maximillian to take over Mexico. Ferdinand and Carlota took over Mexico. The French said, "Oh, the Americans are finished, let's go in." The British with Lord Palmerston – who was in political service for over half a century – didn't want to back the South because he thought, "well, you never can tell. Let's let them fight and kill each other off and maybe there'll be more spoils than we thought left over." *Europe was waiting like wolves in the background.*

The Russians, the Tsarist Russians, who are the same Russians who are there today. It doesn't make any difference what you call them – they are Russians. Sent ships to San Francisco and New York to do a little reconnaissance, to see what the situation was like. And oh yeah, they still owned Alaska and still had claims all the way down to Fort Bragg, California. I mean this is empire building – this is serious business. And if these boys can't hold it together, then fair is fair. All this was happening at the same time.

The Civil War: Gruesome Modernity on Display

In ***the Civil War***, it ***was the most bloody war in history because every battle was just gruesome.***[56] Because it was the first time that technology had caught up with man's unfortunate butchering possibilities. His instincts to kill.

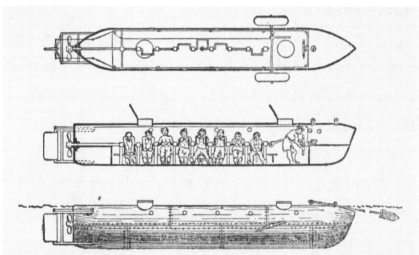

Fig. 1. The Confederate Submarine Boat which Sank the U. S. Steamship 'Housatonic in Charleston Harbor During the Civil War.

The Hunley submarine as depicted in *Popular Science Monthly* (Dec. 1900, p. 159). Source: Internet Archive.

---

[56] The Battle of Antietam (September 17, 1862) has gone down as the bloodiest day in the history of the United States with 22,717 dead, wounded, or missing (James M. McPherson, *Crossroads of Freedom: Antietam, The Battle That Changed the Course of the Civil War*, New York: Oxford University Press, 2002: p. 3).

And ***the Civil War is the first modern war.*** It's the first war where the rifles were sophisticated, where the artillery was sophisticated. It could be used with great accuracy. The Civil War [was] the first time that a submarine sank a ship. The [*USS*] *Housatonic* was blown up in 1864 by a single man in a submarine.[57] It was studied at the time by military theorists and is still studied. If you read military textbooks on strategy, the Civil War battles are still looked at. Robert E. Lee[58] is still held up as a great military genius from whom one can learn.

And it was Robert E. Lee that Lincoln picked to unify the country. And Lee said that he was a Virginian before he was an American. And that Virginia was going to secede. And that he couldn't fight against his kin and his background. And so, Lee went to the South. And the South by this time was learning that the individual states could not survive without some kind of aggregate among themselves, and so, they formed the Confederacy.

---

[57]   The *USS Housatonic* was sunk by the confederate submarine *H. L. Hunley*. The *Hunley* was operated by a crew of nine men – eight 'rowers' and one pilot. More details can be found here: http://bit.ly/history-of-hunley.

[58] Robert E. Lee (1807-1870) is best known as the commander of the army of the Confederate States of America.

Lincoln and McClellan: A Troubled Relationship

Lincoln's problem in the early Civil War was that he depended upon General [George B.] McClellan. And General McClellan's main characteristic was that he bided his time waiting for the right moment to attack. Waiting until his field position was just right.

In one classic battle, he positioned 150 huge giant mortars beautifully so that their shot pattern was going to decimate the enemy. Not one shot was fired because the enemy vacated the position as soon as he got them all set up. They waited several days, let him set the whole thing up, then they just moved. And Robert E. Lee nudged Stonewall Jackson and said, "I believe these boys can be had."

And in fact, the correspondence between Lincoln and McClellan is fraught with concern on Lincoln's part. Why is it, sir, he writes, my ledgers show that you have 120,000 men under arms. And I see by your reports that you're missing somewhere around 50,000 men. Now I understand that there are casualties and deserters and so forth. Say that there are 5,000 that are really unaccountable. Where are these other 45,000 men Sir? What are they doing? If you had these 45,000 men, I believe that you could take Richmond,

Virginia in three days.[59] He would send letters like this to McClellan.[60]

And so, McClellan would get going and say, we've got to get this camp moving. And so, he'd spend the three days getting everybody organized so that the uniforms were right, and the drill was right. And that's how the Civil War dragged on and on and on, until Lincoln relieved McClellan of his command.[61]

And then the command was split. He brought in General [Ambrose E.] Burnside,[62] who fought one battle and lost something like 23,000 killed.[63] And Lincoln pulled him out mercifully right away. The Army of the Potomac was

---

[59] This is a paraphrasing of a letter from President Lincoln to Major General George B. McClellan written on April 9, 1862. See the full transcript here: http://hd.housedivided.dickinson.edu/node/40510.
[60] Another example of this correspondence is a letter from Lincoln to McClellan on October 25, 1862: "I have just read your despatch about sore tongued and fatiegued horses. Will you pardon me for asking what the horses of your army have done since the battle of Antietam that fatigue anything?"
[61] President Lincoln ordered McClellan's removal from command on November 5, 1862. George B. McClellan (1826-1885) would eventually go on to be the presidential nominee for the Democratic party in the 1864 election – facing off against none other than Abraham Lincoln. He would eventually go on to serve as governor of New Jersey (1878-1881).
[62] Major General Ambrose E. Burnside assumed command of the Army of the Potomac on November 9, 1862 after Lincoln relieved McClellan of his command. Burnside's distinctive style of facial hair was known as sideburns – a play on his name.
[63] This was the Battle of Fredericksburg (December 11–15, 1862) which ended in a Confederate victory and Union casualties amounting to 12,653 (killed, wounded, and captured/missing).

completely inoperative. The Army of the Tennessee was the only thing going. The Army of the Cumberland was completely bogged down. They had taken a city called Murfreesboro [Tennessee] and there had been so many casualties on both sides that it took six months for that army to bring itself back up. The only individual who could go places was [Ulysses] S. Grant.[64] And in fact, Grant got going because of a very peculiar situation. There was a Senator from Illinois[65] who was a General by political appointment, and he'd conceived a plan to spring himself into national prominence by taking a group of individuals down the Mississippi River, collecting an army along the banks, and then taking supply barges and shooting straight as an arrow down all the way to New Orleans freeing the Mississippi River.

This is a great strategic step if it could be done, because remember now that the Confederate States stretched all the way to the end of Texas. From Miami to El Paso. So, the

---

[64] Ulysses S. Grant (1822-1885), born Hiram Ulysses Grant, eventually adopted the name Ulysses S. Grant. One version of the story is that he was enrolled at West Point under the name 'Ulysses S. Grant' by mistake and rather than go through the hassle of changing his school records he just adopted the name (Hamlin Garland, *Ulysses S. Grant: His Life and Character*, New York: Doubleday & McClure Co., 1898: p. 30-32).
[65]This is possibly a reference to John A. Logan (1826-1886).

Confederacy was a huge spread. And it also meant that Texas was extremely important.

We don't hear too much about Texas in the Civil War because people still are skittish and don't want to talk about it. Texas outflanked the North. The only free state on the other side of the Mississippi was Kansas, and that had just come in. And there were farmers in Kansas.

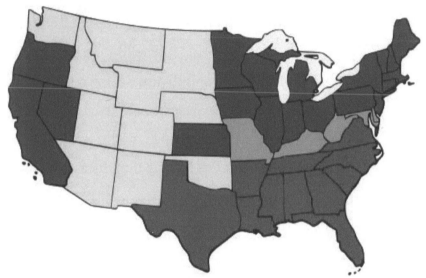

Map showing the Confederacy (red) and the Union (blue). The states identified in light blue (the border states) are slave states that did not secede from the Union. Source: Wikimedia Commons.

But Texas, Texans have always been what they are, fighters. They love to fight. They love to get the boys together in the saddle and get the coal oil torches lit and ride North.

Texas outflanked the North. And if Texas came into the Civil War with its strength there was almost no way that the North was going to be able to hold onto the Midwest. And without the Midwest manpower the economic base of the North would not be able to affect a victory. It would be at the best a stalemate, which would mean that the Confederacy would be able to exist and pull the border states into it, and eventually the Union would be forever doomed.

America: An Experiment on the Verge of Extinction

Lincoln saw this. He saw this as a distinct possibility. That *the United States, as an experiment in democracy, was on the brink of extinction.* And he realized, as Franklin and Jefferson had realized before him, that this is all new ground. That it has never existed in human history anywhere. Mankind doesn't have any experience on this scale. Of turning tens of millions of human beings free and giving them education, background, opportunity, the ability to come together in whatever kinds of groups they want. It has never happened before. And it looked in 1862 as if this was going to be snuffed out.

So, this idea of taking the Mississippi River was a great idea. It would cut the South in half. It would alienate Louisiana and Texas, but especially Texas. So, they couldn't link up to the rest of the South. It would allow for supplies to move [inland]. And for the national economy, which was being focused increasingly in the Midwest.

Remember now, when Lincoln first went to Chicago [in 1847], it had 16,000 people in it. By the 1880s Chicago would have nearly a million people.[66] It just mushroomed all during the Civil War. Hundreds of thousands of people were just pouring in. And so, this Heartland depended upon the Mississippi River traffic for its economic basis.

Grant and Sherman Take the Mississippi Valley

Grant saw this situation. He saw this Senator trying to make a bid for himself. He saw that he wasn't a General. He saw the need to take action. And so, Grant himself arranged for his right-hand man. You know Grant had a right-hand man, just like Lee had Stonewall Jackson. Grant's right-hand man was William Tecumseh Sherman. What they used to call a − excuse my language − a son of a bitch. Sherman was tough. And Grant loved the fact that he could count on Sherman to poke through a situation.

---

[66] In 1850 the city's population was approximately 30,000; by 1870 it was just under 300,000; then by 1890 the population grew to just under 1.1 million (National Academy of Sciences, *Growing Populations, Changing Landscapes: Studies from India, China, and the United States*, Washington, D.C.: The National Academies Press, 2001, p. 281 https://doi.org/10.17226/10144).

So, he sent Sherman North to bring those troops down before this hotshot from Washington could get there to command them. And he brought those troops down and Grant thought that he would meet with Sherman on the Mississippi River. And they figured out that the place that the whole Confederacy in that part of the West, the Mississippi Valley, the one place that held it together was Vicksburg [Mississippi]. And if they could take Vicksburg, they would control the Mississippi River. They would control the destiny of Texas. They would have fractured the Confederacy and they would have given Lincoln a victory, which he needed at this point.

This was late 1862. The war had dragged on and dragged on. There was talk in the North of letting the South go. We don't need them anyway. They're just a problem. There was talk about foreign powers coming in and setting up. So, Lincoln was surrounded on all sides by people getting iffier by the moment.

Another Union Setback: Battle of Chancellorsville

There were no victories that the North could point to. No clear cut victories. Robert E. Lee had managed to prove his military superiority time and time again. Probably one of the greatest demonstrations was at the Battle of Chancellorsville.[67]

He was positioned. He had wanted to go into the North. He was in Maryland and he wanted to go into Pennsylvania. And a huge army, double his size had been brought down. And General [Joseph] Hooker[68] had decided that he was going to outflank Robert E. Lee and come into his position from behind. Lee was in Fredericksburg [Virginia]. And Lee left a token force with a lot of campfires burning. He moved

The Battle of Chancellorsville. Print by Kurz & Allison, 1889. Source: Library of Congress.

---

[67] This battle took place April 30 – May 6, 1863 in Spotsylvania County, Virginia.
[68] Hooker was chosen by Lincoln to replace Burnside.

South; he split his forces into three. He gave the largest of the three forces to Stonewall Jackson. And he took the other forces and they applied a classic pincers move on a superior body of Northern officers at Chancellorsville and decimated them. And then split back and brought their troops together and were all set up for an invasion into the North.

This invasion came about the same time that Grant was laying siege to Vicksburg. And the problem that Grant had with Vicksburg is that Vicksburg was on high bluffs, entrenched with cannon and protected on all of its flanks by strong forts. And Grant tried everything for months to find a way to get to Vicksburg. They tried rechanneling the Mississippi River. Grant said to Sherman, "do you think your boys can dig a new channel for the river?" And Sherman said, "you bet." And in two months they had dug a tremendous channel. Can you imagine that the river perversely would not flow into the new channel? They tried cutting through sandbars and levees. They tried everything to divert the Mississippi, and Old Man River, Old Mystic Man River, will not divert.[69]

They tried to outflank Vicksburg, and every time they came upon a situation. One American phrase comes from

---

[69] This is known as "Grant's Canal"; more information is available on Wikipedia: https://en.wikipedia.org/wiki/Grant's_Canal.

this – "Up the Yazoo." The Yazoo is a river. It's a tributary of the Mississippi [River].[70]

And Grant moved his forces by stealth, these low flat boats up the Yazoo River. And they got up to the very top and there was a Confederate fortress that couldn't be taken. And they had to beat a hasty retreat. The Confederates had cut down trees so that they were laying over the stream and almost trapped the Union Army.

So finally, Grant figured out after about seven months, how to thread this puzzle. It's almost like a classic Chinese puzzle. And he moved his forces South about 50 miles. Managed to get his men by stealth across the Mississippi [River], to a little innocuous landing that didn't have a strong enough force. And made his way in a great big arc over to Jackson, Mississippi, the capital, that lay in the rail line that supplied Vicksburg. And he took Jackson.

And then with Sherman, turned and made a dynamic military plunge along the rail line and took Vicksburg. They took Vicksburg on the 4th of July. And the battle of Gettysburg [Pennsylvania] was over on the 4th of July, the same day. And Vicksburg and Gettysburg should have ended the war, but Lincoln's Generals let him down again.

---

[70] The Yazoo River is located in the states of Louisiana and Mississippi.

They refused to pursue Lee. Refused perhaps is not the diplomatic word. ***Lincoln kept relieving men of duty and putting others in charge. And they just would not understand that this was not an ordinary war. That you cannot just simply take military objectives and expect the other side to capitulate.*** That this is, what we would call today ***archetypal projection.*** And that the only way to break that is to break the enchantment. And as long as they have Robert E. Lee and the Confederate Army, they are never going to give up. And they will sacrifice every man, woman, and child. We will have to kill them all to win. If we do not break the Confederate Army and bring Robert E. Lee to bay because he has become the projection focus. Not Jefferson Davis, but Robert E. Lee had become the focus of the man of the South; the incarnation of the mind of the South. The great defender of our right not to play by their rules. And we're doing all right by ourselves. Lincoln alone was the man who had the capacity to see this necessity. And almost none of his Generals understood.

And so, the Civil War dragged on for another two years. And in Lincoln's words, it could have dragged on indefinitely. Except that he finally had found the right commander in Grant and his buddy Sherman. And so, he began feeding them more supplies, more men.

And of course, we'll go into some of that after our break. I think we need to break now.

Lincoln's Great Speech: The Gettysburg Address

. . . These quotations for you. . . Hundreds of them and get everything set up and then I never get to them. I want to read you – read to you. That's better English. I have here a letter from Lincoln.

Lincoln was [six feet four inches tall] and weighed 180 pounds. Wore a stovepipe hat, but he took it off to read this. He had to wear his glasses when he was blowing a little bit. And he read this in Southern Pennsylvania at Gettysburg:

Four score and seven years ago our fathers brought forth on this continent, a new nation, conceived in Liberty, and dedicated to the proposition that all men are created equal.

Now we are engaged in a great civil war, testing whether that nation, or any nation so conceived and so dedicated, can long endure. We are met on a great battle-field of that war. We have come to dedicate a portion of that field, as a final resting place for those who here gave their lives that that nation might live. It is altogether fitting and proper that we should do this.

But, in a larger sense, we can not dedicate—we can not consecrate—we can not hallow—this ground. The brave men, living and dead, who struggled here, have consecrated it, far above our poor power to add or detract. The world will little note, nor long remember what we say here, but it can never forget what they did here. It is for us the living, rather, to be dedicated here to the unfinished work which they who fought here have thus far so nobly advanced. It is rather for us to be here dedicated to the great task remaining before us—that from these honored dead we take increased devotion to that cause for which they gave the last full measure of devotion—that we here highly resolve that these dead shall not have died in vain—that this nation, under God, shall have a new birth of freedom—and that government of the people, by the people, for the people, shall not perish from the earth.

That was November 19th, 1863. He wrote it out by hand and this is a facsimile of that.[71]

---

[71] An image of the facsimile version has been included in this booklet.

Facsimile of Lincoln's handwritten Gettysburg Address. Source: Library of Congress.

Lincoln's Practice of Government

Lincoln's theory of government was not a theory. It was a practice of government that the only practice of government is *that there should be a unity of all the people, and there should be an individuality of any particular person*. And as long as those two are intact, the current of liberty will flow and make possible whatever can be. Whatever the people decide, that is what the future is. That the government has no plans. That the mind of man has no plans. That the past can lay on the present like some dead hand keeping them back from their own destiny.

Lincoln, time and time again, made the point, we don't know what our [descendants][72] will do, but all that we can do is make it possible for them, the vision that is still barely intact in our time and very close to being extinct and going out.

And he said towards the end of his life, again and again, in various speeches, we have to heal the nation. That there is a healing process that has to come in. Unfortunately, the assassination took away the doctor and the nation has never been healed. Never, never been healed.

---

[72] Roger said 'ancestors', but given the context he clearly meant 'descendants'.

Well, let's see some slides and then next week we're going to come to what came after Lincoln.

Abe and Andy sewing up the divided nation. Drawing by Joseph E. Baker, 1865. Source: Library of Congress.

Slides

Editor's Note:

The following are descriptions of various photos related to the content of this presentation. No documentation exists to indicate the specific photos referenced, therefore the photos included are based on Weir's descriptive information compared with digitized photos available from the Library of Congress, Wikimedia Commons, and other sources where identified.

Slide 1. Abraham Lincoln, Congressman-elect from Illinois, 1846 or 1847 (earliest known photo of Lincoln). Photo by Nicholas H. Shepherd. Source: Library of Congress

Slide 1. This is Abe in 1846. He was born in 1809. So, he's 35 years old. Young lawyer. He never grew a beard until he got into the White House. The day that he took his inauguration in 1861, he put the razor down and didn't shave again. Not a great deal has been made out of this, but I think we should make a little bit out of this. There's something about the purification. It's like a Hercules or a Samson. It's the purification that one will not tend to oneself until the others are taken care of first. Until the other business is done first. Almost all of the descriptions of Lincoln talk about how frumpy he was dressed. That he just didn't seem to care about his personal look. And I think all of that was somewhat of a corollary to this not shaving. That as long as this Civil War drags on his main attention is not to himself, but to use a religious phrase, to the 'flock'. That they need tending before one's self. This is a Bodhisattva notion and one that Lincoln upheld greatly.

Slide 2. Abraham Lincoln, October 27, 1854. Photo by Johan F. Polycarpus von Schneidau. Source: Library of Congress.

Slide 2. A few years later, you can see the tremendous development of character. Look at the bone structure. Let's go back to this. This is a tough frontiersman. Make no doubt about that. Lincoln was tough. That's a tough man. That's somebody who's going to be there tomorrow. There's just no way about it. There's also an *élan*[73] there. There's a direction to move in. There was something to do and it's important. And already we can sense in Lincoln the fact that he's feeling inside of himself the call, as they would say, the call. He didn't quite know yet, how come and why, but he's ready. Whatever. Whenever.

He was homely, but there's a handsomeness to this kind of inner purity. The kind of honesty that this human being is really there for you. And you're not just talking to somebody else, he's there for you. And he had that kind of charisma. And when Lincoln would do his political stumping, he's the first of the great modern politicians who go and shake everybody's hand, call everybody by first name. He's that sort of individual. It's usually said that Andrew Jackson was that

---

[73] *Élan* refers to *élan vital* is a term coined by French philosopher Henri Bergson (1859-1941) in his 1907 book *Creative Evolution*. In the English edition, *Élan vital* was translated as "vital impetus," but is typically understood to mean "vital force." It is a hypothetical explanation for evolution and development of organisms, which Bergson linked closely with consciousness – the intuitive perception of experience and the flow of inner time. (Wikipedia)

kind of a dynamic individual. But Jackson more did his shaking from the back of a horse or something like that. That kind of an individual. Lincoln walked among the people. In fact, we'll see a photograph in here of his home during the election.

Slide 3. Abraham Lincoln, May 7, 1858. Photo by Abraham Byers. Source: Library of Congress.

Slide 3. This is still before getting into the White House. And this is getting closer. This is the late 1850s – 1858. He's beginning to sense by now that some glacial action of history has come to the breaking point. That some large pattern mysteriously has come to the surface. And that he is being put into a position where he may have to step into the traces and pull that off. It's the beginning of the feeling of a man who senses that hard work ahead and he may be the one that has to do it.

Slide 4. Abraham Lincoln, 1858. Photo by Roderick M. Cole.
Source: Library of Congress.

Slide 4. This is during the Lincoln-Douglas debates [1858].

Slide 5. Sarah Bush Johnston Lincoln (December 13, 1788 – April 12, 1869), circa 1865. Source: Charles H. Coleman, *Sarah Bush Lincoln: The Mother Who Survived Him* (Charleston, Illinois: Eastern Illinois State College, 1952): p. 20.

Slide 5. This is his stepmother, Sarah Bush Lincoln. Notice the eyes. Lincoln's look, his focus of eyes. The way in which the personality is seen through the equilibrium of the eyes, is there in the stepmother. She came in when he was about nine years old. He and his sister had lost their mother. Father had gone and remarried and brought this woman and three of her children back. And little Abe rested his head on her stomach when she first came in and she just pulled him and his sister into her heart. Took care of them and nurtured that sense of humor. She had a tremendous sense of humor. It may not look like it here, but just because one is serious about life does not preclude humor.

Slide 6. Mary Todd Lincoln, 1861. Photo by Mathew Brady. Source: Library of Congress.

Slide 6. Mary Todd Lincoln in her best. She would have liked to be seen in her best. These were just bought yesterday. Everything here. They will not be worn again. She was the belle of the ball. The product of Kentucky finishing schools. She knew what she wanted. And Lincoln looked like a goer. She just didn't realize that he was going to go for the stars and not just for some nice property portfolio.

Slide 7. Stephen A. Douglas (1813-1861) between 1850 and 1852. Photo by Mathew Brady. Source: Library of Congress.

Slide 7. This is Stephen Douglas. About a foot shorter than Lincoln.[74]

---

[74] Because of his diminutive height, Douglas was given the nickname 'The Little Giant'.

Slide 8. Horace Greeley, journalist and publisher of the New York Tribune between 1844 and 1860. Photo by Mathew Brady. Source: Library of Congress.

Slide 8. Horace Greeley, the editor, who became an incessant critic of Lincoln. "What is this man doing? Does he know what he's doing? Who knows what Lincoln was doing?"

Slide 9. Lincoln's house, Springfield, Illinois, 1860. Source: Library of Congress.

Slide 9. This is Lincoln's house in Springfield, Illinois downstate. Still available. This is during the election. Lincoln somewhere in the center of that crowd. You get the homey feeling of Lincoln here in this shot. We talked a lot about his universal greatness because we have to. We're in a limited timeframe and so we can't dwell upon it, but the man was lovable. And he was homey. And you can see I think in this shot here, the tremendous sense of family participation. That the individual related almost indistinctly to the family structure. We've lost that in this country by and large. But it used to be very natural. The kind of camaraderie which a family has, which people now are trying to replace by all kinds of cult phenomenon and other kinds of surrogate sociological structures. But the American family at this time was an extremely rough and ready matrix that held together.

Slide 10. Lincoln and his secretaries, John G. Nicolay (left) and John M. Hay (right), November 8, 1863. Photo by Alexander Gardner. Source: Library of Congress.

Slide 10. These are the two secretaries, private secretaries of Lincoln. This is [John G.] Nicolay here and that's John Hay. And we'll see a little bit more of John Hay, next week. John Hay became the best friend of Henry Adams, who we talk about next week. We start with Henry Adams. We have to start with Henry Adams because Adams comes right after Lincoln. Adams is the great grandson of John Adams. Grandson of John Quincy Adams. And the son of John Freer Adams, who was the American ambassador to England during the Civil War. So, Henry will have grown up in this family tradition four generations deep now. And the first thing Adams wants to know as a young man, what happened to this country? And so, he will go back and painstakingly sift through all the evidence and write a huge nine volume *The History of the United States During the Administrations of Jefferson and Madison*.[75] Because like an eagle he will sense that something was here that we have lost. What was it? And Adams will painstakingly try to reassemble the time in historical portraits to find out what is no longer here. And of course, he would find it because it's there.

---

[75]   This publication is more commonly known by the title, *The History of the United States of America, 1801-1817*.

Slide 11.[76] This is Hay and Nicolay, who collected all of Lincoln's writings. And the first great collection of Lincoln's writings was edited by Hay. Hay was an Illinois product also.

Slide 12. Abraham Lincoln, 1861. Photo by Christopher German. Source: Library of Congress.

---

[76] At the time of printing, the editor was unable to locate an image that accurately reflected this description. Thus, there is no accompanying photo for this description.

Slide 12. Here's Lincoln as he came into office, 1861. Starting his beard. He still hasn't been hit you see. There's still no scarring. But you'll see as the face changes now during the next four years, bearing up under the torments, one gets scarred.

Slide 13. Abraham Lincoln, 1861. Photo by Mathew Brady.
Source: Library of Congress.

Slide 13. And here is the portrait that Brady took of Lincoln when he came in about the day after the inauguration. And you can see the tremendous staunchness in his posture. One of the most photographed men of his time. We have about 120 photographs of Lincoln.[77]

---

[77] At the time of printing there are approximately 130 known photographs of Abraham Lincoln in existence (Wikipedia).

Slide 14. General McClellan and President Lincoln (left to right) with Union soldiers at Antietam, October 1862. Photo by Alexander Gardner. Source: Library of Congress.

Slide 14. Here's Lincoln and there's McClellan on the left. That's McClellan right there. And Lincoln is saying, how come you're still here? The enemy is about a hundred miles away.

He's bigger than the whole Army yeah. He incidentally was a great strategist. If you read through it, I [have] marked out for you all the passages. He would send letters to the Generals and tell them look here's this objective. Here are these men. Why don't you organize along these lines and go in there this way and take that objective.

So, Lincoln was really the commander in chief. It's hard to understand. There is a book by T. Harry Williams called *Lincoln and His Generals*. And he shows in that book that Lincoln was a great military strategist. He understood. He's the one that proceeded with the Naval blockade of the South. And finally, if you can imagine blockading the entire seacoast perimeter of the Confederacy. Which was effectively done by January of 1865. There was a tremendous logistic net to lay for 1865.

Slide 15. President Abraham Lincoln, May 16, 1861. Photo by Mathew Brady. Source: Library of Congress.

Slide 15. Now you can see that he's sort of leaning into the chair a little bit more. This is still in 1861. Events are beginning to occur, and the profile here shows the same man with the same determination and patience, but he's carrying a higher tension. He's like a high-grade wire that can carry the current.

Slide 16. President Lincoln delivering his inaugural address on the east portico of the U.S. Capitol, March 4, 1865. Photo by Alexander Gardner. Source: Library of Congress.

Slide 16. This is the second inauguration. And there's Lincoln up in the center giving his speech in the second inaugural. In the first inauguration the dome of the Capitol was unfinished. It was a big pit with just some steel beams. And the photo that I have – it was not very good to make us a slide – but it's ironic that during the first inaugural, the Capitol dome should not be there. It's like the dome of Jefferson's vision was literally not there. It had to be reinstated.

Slide 17. President Abraham Lincoln and Major General George McClellan at Antietam in October 1862. Photo by Mathew Brady. Source: Library of Congress.

Slide 17. Now you can see the wear and tear a little bit more. This is after [Antietam].[78] And there was so much blood on the battlefield that it just soaked the ground. The ground was mud, not from water but from blood. He's having to pursue the war. And you see that it's like being sociologically crucified. The very thing that one would not want to do. To kill one's country by the tens of thousands, by the hundreds of thousands, is the very thing that one must do. It's the worst of all possible destinies. And it's beginning to show. And usually people break here in terms of beginning to fantasize. The greatness of Lincoln is that he did not fantasize. He maintained the vision of the real.

---

[78] In the recording Roger states, "after Shiloh," however there are no known photos of Lincoln from 'after Shiloh'. There are photos of Lincoln 'after Antietam', thus it is the editor's belief that Roger misspoke and meant to say 'Antietam' instead of 'Shiloh'.

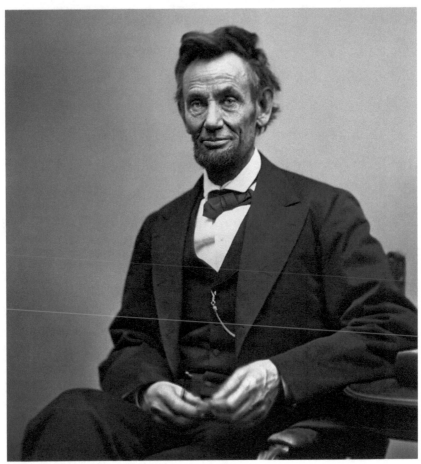

Slide 18. Abraham Lincoln, February 5, 1865. Photo by Alexander Gardner. Source: Library of Congress.

Slide 18. Here's Lincoln towards the end of the Civil War. And I think you can see in the face here the overwhelming humility of being mortal in a situation that requires immortal vision. And yet one is perishing.

You know Lincoln was the first to proclaim Washington's birthday as a sacred holiday. And he said, we have to remember where we came from. And the only way for us to remember that is to look at the people who were there. And that when we see Washington as a human being, what he did. When we see Jefferson as a human being and what he did. These individuals speak to us beyond whatever texts we could refer to. They tell us immediately what we must do. We must maintain our integrity regardless of the situation. And the integrity must be in sync with a vision of the whole. Regardless of the temptations. And that this is the only thread that is real. All the other strands are make-believe. And it's true that we have to juggle and make-believe in order to find some way to get from here to there. But it's all tentative. It's all a raft that has to be abandoned eventually. So, Lincoln has that capacity.

I guess that's it. Well, next week, Henry Adams. And we'll go back to the beginnings.[79]

---

[79] This presentation was part of a 13-part series of presentations entitled *Hermetic America – Our Critical Heritage: James Fenimore Cooper, Abraham Lincoln, Henry Adams, and Mark Twain*. The subsequent presentations on Henry Adams as well as over two thousand others are freely available at https://sharedpresencefoundation.org.

Bio of Roger A. Weir

Roger A. Weir (1940-2018) was an American scholar and lifelong educator. He was born and raised in Saginaw, Michigan. Due to health restrictions as a child he spent much of his time reading – everything from Asimov to Edgar Rice Burroughs. This early reading would ultimately set the stage for a life of dedicated research and education.

Weir received a Bachelor's of Science in philosophy from the University of Wisconsin – Madison in 1963. After graduating he took a couple years off to independently study architecture and Chinese culture. In 1965 he enrolled in a master's program at San Francisco State College (now San Francisco State University). Weir earned a Master's of Arts in Interdisciplinary Studies in 1969.

Shortly after graduating from SF State, Roger was recruited by Mount Royal College (now Mount Royal University) in Calgary to design and teach a special interdisciplinary curriculum. There he created a 16 part curriculum over the course of 5 years, and taught 9 courses himself.

Weir returned to the U.S. in the late 70s, relocating to Los Angeles. Shortly thereafter he began delivering lectures at various venues around the area. Over the next four decades he delivered over two thousand recorded presentations, aided by his growing private library of over 80,000 volumes. The two lectures included in this booklet are just a sampling of Weir's lectures, which run the gamut of civilization, science, and the human experience. Explore more of this content at https://sharedpresencefoundation.org.